MW00937026

Site Notes 1

THE CARNARVON TABLET

George Herbert, 5th Earl of Carnarvon

Site Notes 1

THE CARNARVON TABLET

Bill Petty

Museum Tours Press
Littleton, Colorado

Published by

Museum Tours Press
A division of
Museum Tours, Inc.
7110 Old Farm Road
Littleton, CO 80128

www.museum-tours.com
mt@museum-tours.com

The type fonts used in this book are
Times New Roman and Arial.
Hieroglyphs are derived from several sources including
Saqqara Technologies' Inscribe.

ISBN-13: 978-1523663552
ISBN-10: 1523663553

Book design by Petty
Front Cover Photo – The Carnarvon Tablet

16-1

Contents

Photos

Front Cover – The Carnarvon Tablet
Frontpiece – George Herbert, 5th Earl of Carnarvon
Page
4 top – Lord Carnarvon
bottom – Lord Cromer
5 top – Gaston Maspero
bottom – Arthur Weigall
6 top – Theodore Davis
lower right – W. F. Petrie
lower right – Percy Newberry
7 – Howard Carter
8 – Excavations in the Barabi
9 – First Appearance of the 'Valley'-Temple Wall
10 – F. Ll Griffith
30-31 – The Carnarvon Tablet, front side
32-33 – The Carnarvon Tablet, back side
43-67 – line images of the Carnarvon Tablet, front side
69-79 – line images of the Carnarvon Tablet, back side
Back Cover – 5th Earl of Carnarvon

Note: All photographs used in this book are believed to have been originally published prior to 1923 and are in the public domain. They are all freely available on the internet.

Introduction

This is the first book in the "Site Notes" series. Each book will select a topic to examine, both from an historical context and content. The topic might be an archaeological site, a monument, or any object of special interest.

The Carnarvon Tablet (officially Carnarvon Tablet I) was chosen as the subject of our first book due to its historical interest. This includes the facts surrounding its discovery and the great amount of early speculation and study it engendered. Even with its importance, it is not clear that it has ever been put on public display. The most recently published photograph that I have been able to locate is over 100 years old.

The reader will find several inconsistencies in the spelling and choice of various proper names as well a few common words: Ptah-hotep may be spelled Ptah-hetep, Ptahhopte or Ptahhotep; Precepts may be referred to as Proverbs; vizier may be wizer; and so on. These represent the spellings by the original authors and no attempt has been made to change them.

I hope this book will provide the reader with new information and insights about an important historical artifact.

Enjoy!

.

Bill Petty
February, 2016

Chapter 1

History of the Discovery

History of the Discovery

The Carnarvon Tablet, almost certainly the most important inscription discovered during the first two decades of the 20th century, was found in 1908, but the story of its discovery and the people involved begins a few years earlier.

George Herbert (1866-1923), 5th Earl of Carnarvon, first arrived in Egypt in January 1905. Hereditary peer and owner of a large estate, he was born and raised at Highclere Castle in Hampshire, England. He married well and was able to indulge his hobbies of horses and automobiles. Severely injured in an auto accident in 1901, he never fully recovered. In order to escape the damp cold of English winters he was advised to spend his winters in Egypt, which he did beginning in 1905.

Lord Carnarvon

Egypt was bustling with tourism by the early twentieth century. Thomas Cook & Son was bringing about 50,000 tourists a year from England. Additionally, German, French and Americans were flocking to visit this ancient land. In Luxor, plans were underway to build a grand, new, luxury hotel, to be named the Winter Palace. On his early visits, in 1905 and 1906, Carnarvon played the role of a wealthy tourist, but soon became bored with sightseeing and socializing. His fellow peer, and the Consul-General of Egypt, Evelyn Baring, 1st Earl of Cromer, suggested that excavating for antiquities might provide a pleasant diversion.

Lord Cromer

Lord Cromer (1841-1917) graduated from the Royal Military Academy in 1858, receiving a commission in the Artillery. He resigned after 14 years in the service to become a career diplomat. In 1882, at the age of 41, he was appointed Consul-General of Egypt, from which position he virtually ruled the country. In 1906 he advised Carnarvon to apply to Gaston Maspero, director-general of the department of antiquities in Egypt, for an excavation permit.

Gaston Maspero (1846-1916) was a protégé of the great French Egyptologist Auguste Mariette and twice assumed the position of director-general of the department of antiquities in Egypt, a position always held by a Frenchman. His first term in office saw several important initiatives. He began charging admission for visits to the archaeological sites and initiated controls over what antiquities could legally leave the country. In 1901, during his second term, he established the two positions of Chief Inspector of Upper Egypt and Chief Inspector of Lower Egypt, bringing a level of control and discipline to the excavations, which until that time were being carried out with little or no supervision. Upon the recommendation of Lord Cromer, Maspero issued a permit for Carnarvon to excavate during the 1906 season under the supervision of then chief inspector of Upper Egypt, Arthur Weigall.

Gaston Maspero

Arthur Weigall (1880-1934) had an affinity for languages and was a gentleman, comfortable in the higher echelons of British society. His father had been an officer in the British army who died in action the year Weigall was born. Weigall loathed the private trade in antiquities and believed his job as chief inspector was to oversee the many excavations taking place in his district. Unlike his predecessors, he viewed working with excavators as a conflict of interest. He had a particular distaste for the practice of awarding permits to excavate for antiquities to rich, but unqualified individuals, exemplified by the American, Theodore Davis.

Arthur Weigall

Theodore Davis

Theodore Davis (1837-1915) was a wealthy American lawyer with a love for Egypt and excavation. A complete amateur, he often relied on others, including Howard Carter from 1902 to 1904, to supervise the actual work of excavating. In 1905, Weigall persuaded Davis to acquire the permit to excavate in the Valley of the Kings, but Weigall inserted the requirements that Davis hire a full-time archaeologist to supervise all of the work and that any objects found would belong to the department of antiquities. Davis agreed to these conditions. Eventually Weigall was able to persuade Maspero to apply the requirement that all excavations by amateurs throughout Egypt must have a full-time archaeologist to supervise all work. But it was a policy often ignored if class, politics or money dictated.

W. F. Petrie

Howard Carter (1874-1939) was the son of a painter and had entered Egyptology in 1891 as a tracer of tomb inscriptions. Like Arthur Weigall, Carter was a field educated Egyptologist. Neither man had attended university, both were largely self-taught, and both had a talent for art. Each, at different times, had worked under the tutelage of Percy Newberry (1869-1949) and Sir William Flinders Petrie (1853-1942). Carter was an excellent artist and learned to become an extremely competent excavator. He was also a natural leader and a good administrator, and while often awkward in English society he was comfortable and well liked by the Egyptians. In January, 1900, at the age of 25, Howard Carter was appointed the first Chief Inspector of Upper Egypt (the position that Weigall held in 2006). As Chief Inspector he was excellent at organizing projects, such as introducing electric

Percy Newberry

Howard Carter

lighting to the Valley of the Kings. However, unlike Weigall, Carter did not see his job as just overseeing excavations, but rather working with the excavators. He hired himself out as an excavation supervisor, in which capacity he made several major discoveries. He also acted as a dealer in antiquities, a practice which was perfectly legal at the time, even though it was abhorred by Weigall. In late 1904, Carter was reassigned as Chief Inspector for Lower Egypt. Within a year he was involved in a dispute pitting honor against politics and he resigned from the service. After leaving the department of antiquities in October, 1905, Carter became a free lance artist, working on various commissions in Luxor. Meanwhile, 25 year-old Arthur Weigall had assumed the position of Chief Inspector of Upper Egypt.

Lord Carnarvon had become acquainted with Arthur Weigall in 1905. In late January, 1907, Carnarvon presented Weigall with his permit to excavate and asked to be assigned a site. Because the permit did not contain a provision requiring a qualified archaeologist be on site at all times, Weigall assigned Carnarvon a safe site where he could do no harm. The rubbish mounds at Gurneh were chosen on the grounds that if there was nothing to be found then there was nothing that could be damaged. Carnarvon was conscientious, but unprepared to oversee an excavation. Unlike Davis, however, he was on site daily, supervising the workmen, who had been recruited from the neighboring villages. But there was little to be found in the rubbish mounds and it is unlikely that he would have known how to properly treat any antiquities that he did find. After excavating for six weeks, the only result that Carnarvon had to show for his effort was a mummified cat.

Disappointed with his first season's results, but not at all disillusioned with excavation, Carnarvon went over Weigall's head and negotiated directly with Maspero for a better, more interesting site to excavate during the 2008 season. He also wrote to Weigall, attempting to assuage his fears by telling him that he would bring a professional with him to make up for his own lack of knowledge.

The 2008 season found Carnarvon digging at Dra Abu el Naga, the region between Deir el Bahari on the south and the road leading to the Valley of the Kings on the north. But contrary to the assurances he had given Weigall, there was no experienced archaeologist to supervise the work. In Carnarvon's own words, written in 1912, 4 years after the fact:[1]

Fig. 1. Excavations in the Birabi

"My preliminary excavations eventually resulted in my confining attention to three sites in that part of the necropolis which lies between the dromos leading to Der el Bahari and the great gorge giving entrance to the Valley of the Tombs of the Kings. These three sites were: (1) a spot a few metres to the north of the village mosque, where, according to the natives, lay a hidden tomb; (2) the Birabi, which is near the desert edge, between the hills of Drah abu el Nagga and the cultivated land, and adjoins the entrance to the dromos of Hatshepsut's famous terrace temple ; and (3) that part of the XIth Dynasty cemetery which lies along the hill slope, on the northern side of the Der el Bahari valley.

"Excavation on the first site was begun in 1908, and, after a fortnight's arduous work among the native houses and rubbish heaps of the village, an important inscribed tomb of the beginning of the XVIIth Dynasty was opened. This tomb proved to be of a 'King's Son' named Teta-Ky, and contained, among many painted scenes, a figure of Aahmes-nefert-ari, the queen of Aahmes I and mother of Amenhetep I. This is the earliest known portrait of the celebrated queen, who afterwards became the patron goddess of the necropolis: she is figured as of fair complexion and not black, as is usually the case in her portraits of a later date. The scene shows her adoring the goddess Hathor, as a cow issuing from a cliff; and behind her is a lady, presumably the queen's mother, named Teta-hemt, who is otherwise unknown. In the course of clearing this tomb many wooden Funerary Figures, in model coffins, were brought to light. These figures were of two types: (1) rudely carved mummiform figures with model coffins of wood,

Fig. 2. First Appearance of the 'Valley'-Temple Wall

clay, or pottery, some of which were inscribed with hieratic or linear hieroglyphic texts; and (2) well-carved figures in wood, painted and with gilt faces, and inscribed with an early form of Chapter VI of the Book of the Dead. The figures of the first type were all found in the four niches in the courtyard wall. Those of the second type were buried in pairs in shallow holes round the four sides of the top of the main pit shaft in the centre of the courtyard floor. The placing of shawabti figures in this position—as it were for them to guard the mouth of the pit of the sarcophagus chamber—is only known in this instance.

"The clearance of Teta-Ky's tomb having been completed, we turned our attention to the Birabi site. Three days' digging in the loose debris unmasked a hidden burial-place. Masses of pottery and denuded mummies were brought to light, and at the very threshold of the tomb (afterwards numbered 9) were discovered two wooden tablets (one in fragments) covered with stucco and inscribed with hieratic texts. One of these tablets has written (1) on its obverse, an important historical text relating to the expulsion of the Hyksos kings by the King Kamosi; and (2) on its reverse, a copy of part of the well-known Precepts of Ptah-hetep."

Of course, at the time, Carnarvon had no idea of the importance of his discovery as he had no qualified person on site to inform him. When Carnarvon's excavation season came to an end, it happened that the Chief Inspector, Weigall, was away from Luxor. Thus, Carnarvon gathered all the antiquities he had found and left them in Weigall's office. Among other items these included: a canopic box, 3 canopic jars, several unbroken pieces of pottery, and a basket full of lesser objects. Included in the basket was the tablet, broken and chipped, with some of the text flaked off. Whether it was damaged when found, or had been damaged through rough handling by Carnarvon or his workmen is not known.

Upon his return to Luxor, Weigall immediately recognized the importance of the tablet. Even if he was unable to completely read the hieratic script he would surely have recognized the date at the beginning of line 1 and the cartouches on lines 2 and 10. In any event he had the tablet photographed, and sent the pictures to England, to Francis Llewellyn Griffith, editor of the Egypt Exploration Fund's archaeological reports. The tablet itself, along with the other finds, was then sent to the antiquities department in Cairo.

F. Ll. Griffith

Francis Llewellyn Griffith (1862-1934) had attended the University of Oxford, where, due to the lack of a specialized department, he taught himself Egyptology. At the urging of one of his professors he sought, and was accepted, to train in Egypt under Petrie (like both Carter and Weigall). After a post in Egyptology was established at Oxford, Griffith was appointed Reader, a position between Associate Professor and Full Professor, in 1901.

Griffith translated the tablet and wrote to Weigall, commenting on the condition of the tablet. On October 1, Weigall replied,[2]

"I am sure . . . rough handling is responsible for some of the flaking. A sadder instance of the sin of allowing amateurs to dig could not be found."

To which Griffith answered,[3]

"It is grievous to think the plaque may have been perfect when found."

In any event, at Maspero's encouragement, or perhaps insistence, Carnarvon hired Howard Carter to be his "learned man" for all of his future excavations, which ultimately led, in 1922, to the discovery of the tomb of King Tutankhamun.

Over the next several years Carnarvon Tablet I, as it came to be called, caused great interest in the Egyptological community. It was officially published in 1912, in the book, "Five Years Exploration at Thebes," by Carnarvon and Carter. In this publication Griffith wrote a chapter on the tablet in which he presented a description of the tablet along with a partial translation, incorrectly dating it to year 7 of Kamose's reign. It also included a photograph of the tablet, possibly the same that was sent by Weigall to Griffith several years previously.

Sides were taken as to when the text on the tablet was actually written and whether it was a historical narrative or fiction. Gaston Maspero was of the opinion, based on the cursive style, that it had been written around the 20th Dynasty (See page 9). Raymond Weill, in a 1913 article declared his belief that the tablet was early 18th Dynasty, but that the story was wholly fictional (See page 13). Percy Newberry was emphatic that the document was "exact history" and dated to the 18th Dynasty (See page 13). Alan H. Gardiner (1879-1963), a noted expert on Egyptian philology, opined that the tablet dated from the late 17th or early 18th Dynasty and represented real history (See page 15), boldly stating that,

"the Carnarvon Tablet presents all the customary characteristics of the stelae erected in the temples by the Pharaohs in order to commemorate their good deeds or victorious campaigns. . . . It is by no means unlikely that the text of the tablet is a direct copy from a stele set up by Kamose in one of the Theban temples."

This history/fiction conflict was finally resolved some twenty years later when two stone fragments from a 17th Dynasty stele were discovered in Karnak Temple by H. Chevrier during reconstruction work on the third pylon. Much of the text on the fragments was almost identical to a significant amount of the text on the tablet, confirming Gardiner's speculation.

According to Gardiner, the Carnarvon Tablet, was the most important inscription discovered during the early 20th century. Currently, as of March, 2016, it is being kept in a storeroom at the Grand Egyptian Museum in Giza with the following record:

- **Title,** Tablet: Instructions of Ptahhotep, Hyksos under Kamose
- **Material,** Wood
- **Width,** 25cm
- **Length/Depth,** 51cm
- **Area,** Thebes: West bank, Diospolis Magnai Luxor
- **Site,** Sheikh Abdel-Qurna
- **Period,** New kingdom, Dynasty 18
- **Source,** Excavated by lord Carnarvon in 1910
- **Current location,** Storage (GEM BOX) Grand Egyptian Museum (Under construction)
- **ID number,** JE 41790 - CG 25268

Notes:

1 THE EARL OF CARNARVON, *Five Years' Explorations at Thebes,* London, 1912, pp 2-4.

2. JULIE HANKEY, *A Passion for Egypt: Arthur Weigall, Tutankhamun and the 'Curse of the Pharaohs',* Tauris Parke Paperbacks, London, 2007, pg 127.

3. JULIE HANKEY, *A Passion for Egypt,* Tauris Parke Paperbacks, London, 2007, pg 127.

Chapter 2

Major Publications

1909 - Recueil by Gaston Maspero

The first publication of the tablet (or a portion thereof) appears to be by Gaston Maspero in "Recueil de Travaux Relatifs a la Philologie et a L'Archeologie", Volume XXXI, dated 1909, just one year after the tablet's discovery.[1]

"In the month of February last year, the Earl of Carnarvon, rummaging at Thebes in the mountain of Dra Abu el Naga, collected there, from among the rubble of previous excavations, two pieces of a writing tablet, covered on both sides with texts and drawings. It was one of many items that had been given to the deceased to accompany him into the after-life, and it was killed by breaking it into two, in order that its double could serve its owner's double. This tablet probably represented the library and recreation for its owner. It reads, on one side, the beginning of a semi-historical tale, the action happening in Year 3 of the Pharaoh Kamosis of the seventeenth dynasty, and gives the full original draft for the first time, to my knowledge. It seems to me that this is the first appearance of the history of these times, fragments of which have been preserved for us on various ostraca,[2] but that is not quite certain. On the other side, the scribe had traced a broad outline figure of a game board with four names in the usual squares. This was so that the deceased could play draughts without much effort, when the urge took him. Above this sketch are eight long lines of writing, pressed against each other, containing the first lines of a very-old, moral treatise, the manuscript of which Prisse d'Avennes gave to our National Library, and which Chabas called the world's oldest book. A story, a handbook of practical philosophy, a game board; the dead man had something to distract him forever.

"He had lived probably about the time of the twentieth dynasty, as the writing style of his text seems to be related to the cursive hand of that time rather than to those of the eighteenth. It is small, a bit squarish, quick, with a tendency to turn back at the end, with some characters taking on an almost demotic look. The scribe was quite skilled, but he did not apply more effort than necessary and one can easily understand this, since both the works were destined to remain forever in the darkness of the tomb. The text itself is full of clerical errors, and above all, it is so different from the Papyrus Prisse, that in truth one would sometimes think one was reading a new version rather than a copy of the already known version."

This is followed by a transcription and translation of the Precepts of Ptah-hotep from the tablet, along with a comparison to that found on Papyrus Prisse

1911 - Le Papyrus Prisse et ses Variantes by Gustave Jequier

In 1911, the publication, "Le Papyrus Prisse et ses Variantes" contained a section on "Tablette Carnarvon au Musée du Caire" by Gustave Jéquier and included a full sized print of the text of the Precepts of Ptah-hotep along with the following description.[3]

"A large scribal tablet, found in 1909 in Dra Abu el Naga during excavations of Lord Carnarvon, presents a duplicate of another portion of the Prisse Papyrus, the first lines of the Precepts of Ptahhotep . Thanks to the kindness of Lord Carnarvon, Mr. Griffith and Mr. Gardiner, who are to publish the full results of these excavations, I am able to include a facsimile of the text in question in this work, from a photograph by Mr. Gardiner, enlarged to the exact size of the original, which is now preserved in the Cairo Museum (Entry no. 41790). I offer these gentlemen my sincere thanks for kindly allowing me to complete my work.

"The tablet is quite large (51cm by 25cm), wooden, covered with a layer of stucco, which is now yellowish, well polished and prepared to receive the writing. It is broken lengthwise and the stucco has been somewhat chipped around the break, resulting in the loss of some signs. It was probably a funerary object, undoubtedly that of the scribe who had used it during his life. To this end, he had written two texts that were to serve as recreation in his grave, after his death. On one side is a historical tale, an episode of the war against the Hyksos, and on the other is the beginning of a collection of moral precepts, which was reduced to only eight lines. Below this is the quickly drawn pattern of a game board.

"The writing is drawn in the longitudinal direction of the tablet, in straight and evenly spaced lines, denoting a skillful scribe, at least in terms of calligraphy. As for the paleographic character of this beautiful cursive, firm and legible, Mr. Maspero believes that it belonging to the Twentieth Dynasty, while Mr. Gardiner, in response to various findings that probably issue from elsewhere, attributes it instead to the Hyksos period .

"As for the text itself, when we compare the Prisse Papyrus (IV.1-V.8) with this latest version, we find no less significant differences than are found with the fragments in the British Museum, which do not contain the early Precepts of Ptahhotep. It is therefore impossible to know if we have three different versions of the precepts in question, or only two, on the one hand the Prisse Papyrus, and on the other the Cairo tablet for the beginning and the fragments in London for the middle and the end. The issue of the difference between the Prisse Papyrus and the tablet from Dra Abu el Naga has been studied very carefully by Mr. Maspero who first gave a transcription and translation of the new text."[4]

1912 - Five Years Exploration at Thebes by Lord Carnarvon

The official publication of the discovery was issued in 1912 in "Five Years Exploration at Thebes: A Record of the Work Done 1907-1911" by The Earl of Carnarvon and Howard Carter. Chapter VI of this book, written by Francis Llewellyn Griffith, contained the following description.

"The writing tablet (Carnarvon Tablet I) is a document of the highest historical importance, preserving as it does a contemporary record of the conflict of the Theban Dynasty with the Hyksos. On the face of the tablet eight lines of hieratic contain the introduction to the famous Proverbs of Ptah-hetep, setting forth how the Wazir Ptah-hetep, son of a king, spoke to his King Assa of the advance of old age upon him and the diminution of all his powers, and requested that he might delegate his duties to his son, whom he would instruct in the words and ways of the Ancients. The King accorded his request and bade him proceed, and thus originated the rules of good conduct which go by the name of the old Wazir. The text[5] of the tablet shows some considerable differences of reading from the only other copy known—that in the Prisse Papyrus.

"Below this fragment of philosophy are marked the lines of a draught-board, in squares 10 x 3. Four of the compartments contain hieratic signs indicating their place in the game.

"The historical text on the other side consisted of no less than seventeen long lines. Unhappily the flaking of the stucco[6] about the fracture has robbed us of one line and of the greater part of two more. The text is singularly difficult, and this great gap, added to some minor imperfections, further obscures the meaning."

Here follows Griffith's rough translation of the text. He ends with,

"It is remarkable that the titles of Kamosi as given do not agree with those upon the Treasure of Ahhotp; the handwriting proves that Lord Carnarvon's tablet (Carnarvon Tablet I) had been written within a few years of the events recorded in it. The publication of the facsimile is certain to rouse the interest of every student of one of the most fascinating problems in oriental history."

1916 - The Defeat of the Hyksos by Alan Gardiner

Finally, Alan H. Gardiner published the "Defeat of the Hyksos by Kamose: the Carnarvon Tablet, No I" in "The Journal of Egyptian Archaeology," Vol 3, No. 2.3, 1916.

"No single inscription has been discovered in the course of the past ten years more important than the writing-board recording a defeat of the Hyksos by the Theban king Kamose, which was found by Lord CARNARVON in 1908, and subsequently published in the fine memoir dealing with his excavations.[7] In that work good photographs of both recto and verso are given, and Mr F. Ll. GRIFFITH contributes a valuable description; but the former are on too small a scale, and the latter is too summary, to satisfy the requirements of the philologist and the historian. On the whole there seems in this case to be sufficient reason for departing from the custom of our Journal, which as a rule is concerned more with the results of Egyptological research than with the technical processes by which these are obtained. The palaeographical interest of the original is very great, and for this reason I have ventured to reproduce the large-scale photographs made for me in 1910 by Herr KOCH; scholars will thus have better means of controlling my readings, some of which are by no means as certain as I could have wished.

"The Carnarvon Tablet no. I belongs to a pair of hieratic writing-boards found among loose debris of pottery and fragmentary mummies on a ledge near the entrance to a plundered tomb in the Birabi, not far from the mouth of the Deir el Bahari valley.[8] The tomb in question is assigned by Mr Howard CARTER to the Seventeenth Dynasty, and we have every reason to believe that this attribution is correct. The two writing-boards are of a type not uncommon at this period, consisting of wooden tablets covered with stucco of fine plaster and having, in the middle of one of the shorter sides, a hole by means of which they could be hung up. Tablet no. I bears on the obverse the historical text here to be considered, and on the reverse first a new copy of the beginning of the well-known *Proverbs of Ptahhotpe* [9] and below this the lines of a draughtsboard in squares 10 x 3. . . .

"The circumstances of the find would predispose one to attribute these writing-boards to the Seventeenth, or at the very latest, to the beginning of the Eighteenth Dynasty. Sir Gaston MASPERO, however, in commenting on the above-mentioned duplicate of the *Proverbs of Ptahhotpe*, expresses the opinion that the scribe by whom this was written lived towards the time of the Twentieth Dynasty, 'car l'écriture de son livre semble se rattacher aux mains cursives de cette époque plutôt qu'a celles de la XVIIIe,' and he therefore draws the conclusion that the text of the obverse represents 'le commencement d'un conte a demi historique, dont l'action se passait dans l'an III du Pharaon Kam6sis de la XVIIIe dynastie.' M. le capitaine R. WEILL, in an interesting but wholly unconvincing treatise on the documentary evidence for the Hyksos period,[10] similarly disputes the historical character of the Carnarvon Tablet, though admitting that it may date back as early as the beginning of the Eighteenth Dynasty. Professor NEWBERRY, on the other hand, declares emphatically that this document 'is certainly not a tale (as has been suggested) but deals with exact history, and if we compare it with the so-called 'Tale of Apepy and Seqenenre' preserved in the Sallier Papyrus no. II (sic, lege no. I), we find some points which lend colour to the old theory that this Sallier Papyrus no. II is a copy of an earlier historical document, and not simply a popular romance.[11] "Though it is impossible to agree with Professor NEWBERRY as regards this latter point, he is undoubtedly right in stating that the hieratic writing is that 'characteristic of the end of the XVIIIth Dynasty.' This verdict is thoroughly borne out alike by its general appearance and by a detailed scrutiny of its individual forms. There is the same love of rounded shapes and terminal flourishes which we find in the Rhind Mathematical Papyrus, the Westcar and the Papyrus Ebers. For the minuter differences of form which distinguish this group of manuscripts, ranging from the beginning of the Hyksos period down to the reign of Amenophis I, from those of later date, reference must be made to Dr MOLLER'S standard work on hieratic palaeography;[12] . . .

"It may be considered certain, therefore, that the Carnarvon Tablet no. I is very nearly contemporary with the events it records; in no case can it have been written more than fifty years later. The question as to its value as a historical document is better deferred until we have become acquainted with the contents."

At this point Gardiner transcribes and translates the Hyksos inscription on the tablet, after which he concludes,

"In attempting to estimate the historical value of this text it appears to me that the question of the date at which it was written is of far greater importance than the question as to the literary category in which it is to be classed. If, as I believe with Mr GRIFFITH and Professor NEWBERRY, the actual writing dates from within a few years of the time when the events recorded are supposed to have taken place, it is surely incredible that those events should be wholly fictitious. The impression that I gain from the narrative does not agree in the least with that which it appears to have made upon M. WEILL :-'Mais si les caractères paléographiques de cet ordre doivent être pris en considération, ils ne sauraient, dans le cas actuel, prévaloir contre un fait pour ainsi dire immédiat, et qui ressort avec évidence de la seule lecture du document, a savoir, qu'il fut composé postérieurement a la victoire définitive des Thébains sur les Septentrionaux.'[13] For my part, I am unable to discover any word or phrase which indicates or implies that the writer was aware of the subsequent taking of Avaris and of the ultimate triumph of the Thebans. On the contrary, unless the text in its complete form, against the custom of early times, was as long and circumstantial as the stele of the Ethiopian Piankhi, the detailed description which the Carnarvon tablet gives of the taking of Nefrusi would surely have appeared ridiculously long and out of proportion in the light of the far more important events that followed. Be this as it may, it is impossible to assent to M. WEILL'S central proposition, which is that the references to Avaris and to the Asiatics here are merely the conventional *clichés* of triumphal proclamations of the Eighteenth Dynasty, and as such without historical value. Much space that cannot here be spared would be required to do justice to M. WEILL'S complicated thesis. I would merely state that, in my opinion, he altogether overshoots the mark in his ultra-sceptical analysis of our sources; a wholly uncritical acceptance of the letter of their text would, I am convinced, give a better idea of the real historical facts than is obtained by such hypercritical methods.

"M. WEILL has, however, rightly perceived[14] that the Carnarvon Tablet belongs to the same category of texts as the great stele of Tutankhamun discovered by M. LEGRAIN at Karnak, though how he reconciles this view with his opinion that it is posterior to the taking of Avaris, i.e. posterior to the reign of Kamose himself, is not apparent. In point of fact, the Carnarvon Tablet presents all the customary characteristics of the stelae erected in the temples by the Pharaohs in order to commemorate their good deeds or victorious campaigns. On such stelae it is quite usual for the Pharaoh to be represented in debate with his ministers, whose advice often amounts to mere flattering approval of the king's own project, though sometimes, as here, they urge a less daring course of action than the Pharaoh himself proposes and subsequently carries out.[15] It is by no means unlikely that the text of the tablet is a direct copy from a stele set up by Kamose in one of the Theban temples. There are irregularities in the first line, which suggests that this may have been adapted from the descriptive epithets accompanying the scene of worship regularly found within the rounded upper portion of commemorative stelae. We may picture to ourselves the figure of Kamose standing before Amun, the royal and the divine titles being engraved above their respective owners' heads; between the two, and at the very top, may have been seen the regnal date. This particular stele may have appealed to the writer of the Carnarvon Tablet on account of the boldness of its metaphors or some other pleasing features in its style. That his motive in making the copy was a literary one may be concluded from the facts that the reverse bears the beginning of the Proverbs of Ptahhotpe and that the smaller tablet also contained a moral tractate. It does not, however, follow that the purpose of the original was the same as that of the copy. The best analogy for what has taken place here will be found in a parchment document, inscribed in hieratic, now in Berlin:[16] this records certain buildings made by Senwosret I at Heliopolis and is a copy made at the time of the Eighteenth Dynasty; the intrinsic interest, apart from the language, makes it impossible to regard this as a romance, and there is, accordingly, reasonable ground for supposing that the original was an authentic commemorative stele. For a similar reason we must reject M. MASPERO'S view that the Carnarvon Tablet contains the beginning of a semi-historical tale; Egyptian tales, as we know them, deal with subjects far more fantastic than mere descriptions of warlike operations.

"There appears, therefore, to be no reason why we should not give just as much credence to the narrative of the Carnarvon Tablet as to any other official Egyptian commemorative stele. No doubt this kind of historical source is not all that could be desired, but since we can neither contradict nor qualify its statements we must make shift with them as best we may. In point of fact, the information that we obtain from the Carnarvon Tablet agrees very well with our previous views on the Hyksos period. In the romance of the Sallier papyrus Seqnenre is a more or less obedient vassal of the Hyksos ruler Apophis. Kamose was probably the immediate predecessor of Amosis I, since both are associated together in the famous find of jewellery and on an inscription at Toshkeh in Lower Nubia.[17] From the tomb of Ahmose at El Kab we learn that Amosis I drove the Hyksos out of Avaris and subsequently defeated them, after a long siege, at Sharuhen in Judah. The movement of which this defeat signalized the triumphant ending may have been the direct and unbroken continuation of the more modest campaign undertaken by Kamose. The utmost limit of Kamose's ambition seems to have been the re-capture of Memphis (1. 4); whether it was he or Amosis to whom that honour fell is not yet known to us.

"Professor NEWBERRY has discussed the name of the conquered foe and the geography of the tablet with his usual acumen and historical insight.[18] Teti he shows to have been a familiar name in the Seventeenth and early Eighteenth Dynasties, and Piopi to be merely a variant form of Apopi, Apophis. Thus Teti, son of Piopi, may have been the son of one of the Hyksos rulers called Apophis, probably the last of them. Professor NEWBERRY notes that the prominence of Cusae in the narrative of the tablet agrees with the statements of the inscription set up by Hatshepsut at Speos Artemidos. There the famous queen describes her restoration of various temples ruined at the time when the Asiatics were in the land, and the temple of Cusae is the southernmost that she mentions. Later, in the Eighteenth Dynasty, the province known as  or Southern Egypt appears to have had its northern boundary a little above Cusae, and it may have been for this reason that the Hyksos deliberately placed their boundary there. It is true that a lintel of an Apophis and a block of Khian have been found at Gebelen, some distance south of Thebes; but it is far from certain that the Hyksos domination ever actually extended as far as there.

"Not the least interesting point about the Carnarvon Tablet is its allusion to a powerful prince in Kush, who claimed equality with the Theban Pharaoh. This reference is confirmed by the biography of Ahmose of El Kab, whence we learn that the defeat of the Hyksos at Sharuhen was immediately followed by a Nubian campaign, where 'His Majesty made a great slaughter' and Ahmose earned for the second time the reward of gold given to doughty warriors."

Notes:

1. The text was translated from the French by Google Translator and edited by Petty.
2. *Contes populaires de l'Ancienne Egypte*, 3e ed., p 231sqq.
3. The text was translated from the French by Google Translator and edited by Petty.
4. Recueil de Travaux relatifs à l'archéol. et à la phil. ég. etass., XXXI , p. 146-153.
5. Jequier, Le Papyrus Prisse et ses variantes (Pap. Brit. Mus. 10371 and 10435, Tablette Carnarvon au Caire), Paris, 1910; Maspero, Recueil, Vol. XXXI, p. 146.
6. The tablet is made of wood covered with stucco of fine plaster for a writing surface.
7. THE EARL OF CARNARVON and HOWARD CARTER, *Five Years' Explorations at Thebes,* London, 1912, pl. xxvii, xxviii, and pp. 36-7.
8. *Op. cit.*, p. 4 and p. 35.
9. See G. MASPERO, *L'Ostracon Carnarvon et le Papyrus Prisse*, in *Rec. de Trav*., vol. 31 (1909), pp. 146-153. Another transcription in E. A. W. BUDGE, *Egyptian Hieratic Papyri*, London, 1910, pp. xviii-xix. A large-scale photographic facsimile in G. JEQUIER, *Le Papyrus Prisse et ses variantes*, Paris, 1911, pl. 16.
10. R. WEILL, *Les Hyksos et la restauration nationale*, Paris, 1911; appeared first in *Journal Asiatique*, 10th series, vols. 16 (1910) and 17 (1911). The Carnarvon Tablet is discussed in an additional article published *Journal Asiatique*, 11th series, vol. I (1913), pp. 536-544.
11. P. E. NEWBERRY, *Notes on the Carnarvon Tablet No. I*, in *Proc. S.B.A.*, vol. 35 (1913), pp. 117-122.
12. G. MOLLER, *Hieratische Palaographie*: I, *Alt- und Mittelhieratisch*; II, *Neuhieratisch*. Leipzig, 1909.
13. *Journal Asiatique*, eleventh series, vol. I (1913), p. 542.
14. *Op. cit.* p. 540.
15. So in the Annals of Tuthmosis III, see BREASTED, *Ancient Records*, vol. II, §§ 420-1.
16. See BREASTED, *Ancient Records*, vol. I, §§ 498-506.
17. WEILL, *Les Hyksos*, pp. 150-2.
18. *Proc. S. B. A.*, vol. 35 (1913), pp. 117-122.

Major Publications

Chapter 3

The Tablet

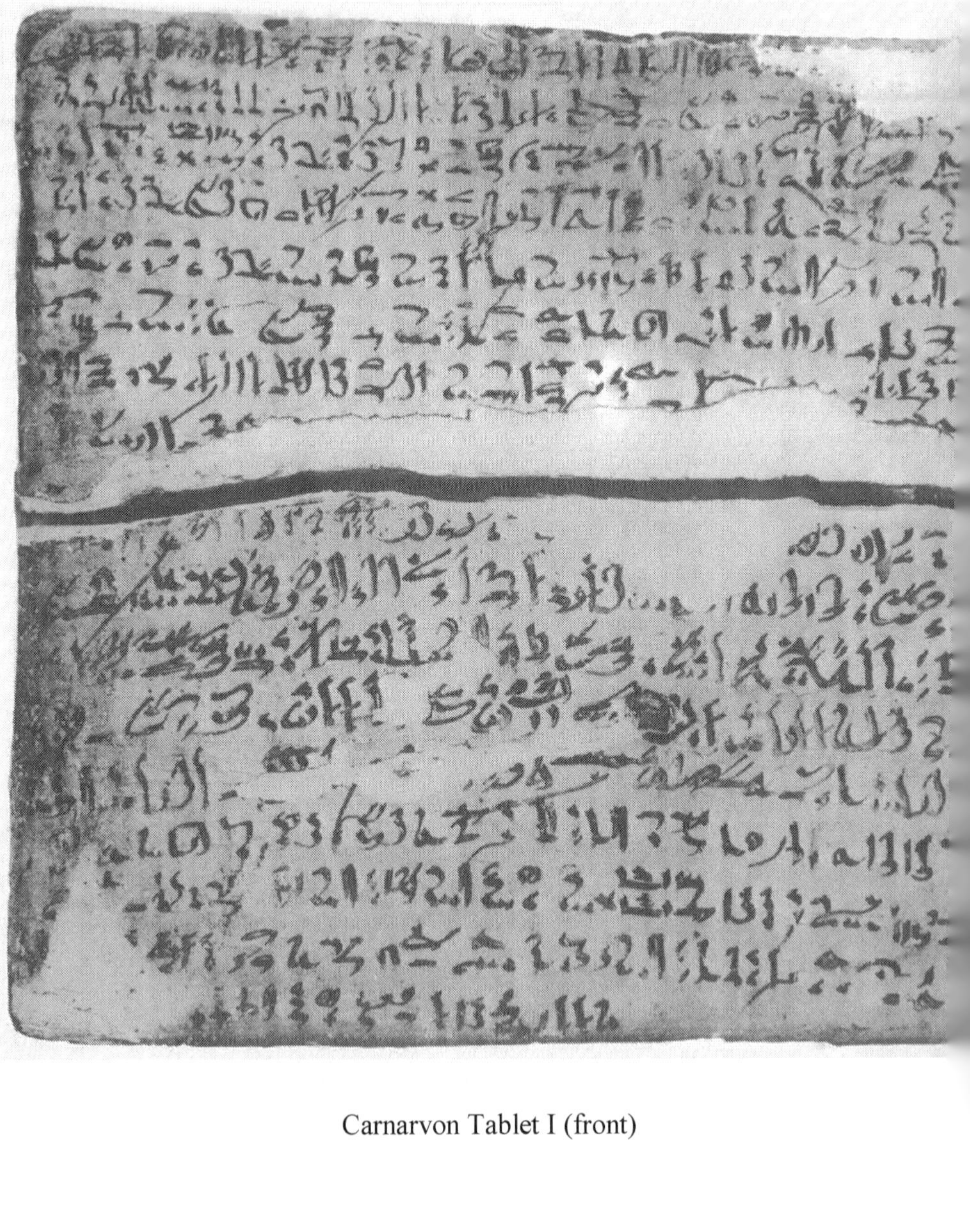

Carnarvon Tablet I (front)

Carnarvon Tablet I (back)

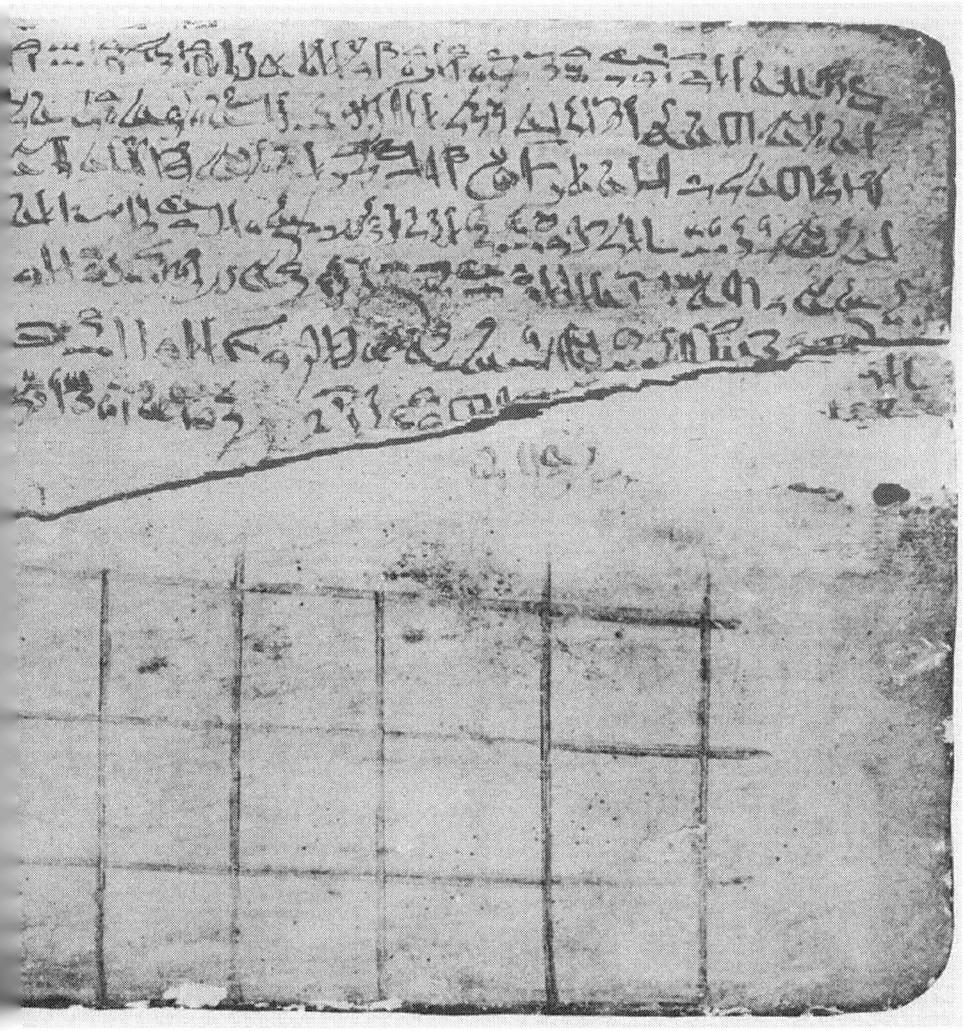

Chapter 4

Translation

Carnarvon Tablet I (Front)

The text that follows is based partly on independent translations of the original tablet by John A. Wilson, Alan H. Gardiner, Hans Wolfgang Helck and Donald Redford. Never-the-less, the end result is strictly that of the author and any errors are his alone. Words in italic indicate words missing from the original text, either because of damage, error, or convention (excluding *the, an, a, of, and, or, but, am, is, are, will, has*). Numbers in parenthesis refer to line numbers of the original text on the tablet.

(1) Regnal year 3; Horus, appearing upon his throne; Two Ladies, repeating monuments; Golden Horus, brings peace to the Two Lands; King of Upper and Lower Egypt; *Wadj*-kheper-*Re, Son of Re*; Kamose, given life - beloved of Amon-Re, Lord of the Thrones of the Two Lands - like Re forever and ever.

(2) The victorious king within Thebes, Kamose, given life forever as an excellent king, because *Re* appointed him king, himself, and has bequeathed to him indisputable strength.

His majesty spoke in his palace to the council of noblemen who

(3) were in his presence:

"I realize what my strength is for. A prince is in Avaris[1] and, another one is in Kush[2], and *here* I sit. I am united with an Asiatic and a Nubian! Each man is in possession of his portion of this Egypt, sharing the land with me.

(4) I cannot pass through it down to Memphis, *on* Egyptian waters. Behold, he possesses Hermopolis[3]. No man can rest, being devastated by the actions of the Asiatics. I will engage with him and I will slit open his belly! My desire is to deliver Egypt and smite

(5) the Asiatics!"

The noblemen of his council spoke, "Behold, The water belongs to the Asiatics beginning at Cusae[4]."

They spoke with one voice, "We have our peace and our portion of Egypt. Elephant-

(6) ine is strong, and the middle *of the land* is united with us as far as Cusae. The finest of their fields are plowed for us. Our cattle and herders are *pastured* in the Delta. Emmer[5] is sent to our swine. Our cattle are not taken by the crocodile.

(7) . . . in it. He is in possession of the land of the Asiatics and we are in possession of Egypt. *Now* then, *if* someone comes and acts against us, then we will act against him!"

Their very presence was painful to the heart of his Majesty.

"As for your advice, . . .

(8) . . . me. I do not respect *he who* shares the land with me. Respect . . . these Asiatics

(9) who . . . from him. I will sail north to do battle with the Asiatics. Success will come. If he thinks about relief from . . . his two eyes with weeping. The entire land will *proclaim*

(10) *me rul*er within Thebes, Kamose, protector of Egypt!"

I sailed north in my strength to drive back the Asiatics as Amon, eminent of counsels commanded. My valiant army

(11) was before me like a hot blast of fire. The Medjay [6] troops were on the top of our *boat's* cabin, to search for the Asiatics and to destroy their positions. The east side and west side *of the river* were bountiful, thereby

(12) the army was (kept) in provisions of food with things from everywhere. I sent forth the victorious Medjay troops. I spent the day day on an expedition to entrap and to punish

(13) Teti, the son of Apepi[7], within Nefrusi[8]. I did not permit him top escape being restrained by me. The Asiatic disrespector of Egypt had made Nefrusi a captive Asiatic nest. I spent

(14) the night in my boat. My heart was happy. When daylight arrived, I was on him like a falcon. By the time of the noon meal I had defeated him. I laid waste his walls, I killed his people and I caused his wife to come down

(15) to the riverbank *in submission*. My soldiers were like lions with their prey, carrying off servants, cattle, milk, fat and honey. Through a division of their possessions, they were happy. The region of Ne*frusi*

(16) had fallen. We were not weary of restrained. Lo, spirits were soaring.

Pershaq[9] was deserted when I arrived at it. Their chariotry was fleeing for home. The guards *likewise*. The mem-

(17) ory of them was obliterated. Their property was . . .

Notes:

1. Kush is south of the first cataract.
2. Avaris was the Hyksos capital in the delta.
3. Hermopol is about 150 miles south of Memphis.
4. Cusae is about 25 miles south of Hermopolis.
5. Emmer wheat was grown primarily in the Delta.
6. The Medjay were elite soldiers, originally from Nubia.
7. "Son of Apepi" was likely an honorific title.
8. The actual location of Nefrusi is unknown but it was almost certainly a little north Cusae.
9. The location of Pershaq is unknown.

Carnarvon Tablet I (Back)

The text that follows is based partly on the translation of the original tablet by Gaston Maspero and others. However, the end result is strictly that of the author and any errors are his alone. Words in italic indicate words missing from the original text, either because of damage, error, or convention (excluding *the, an, a, of, and, or, but, am, is, are, will, has*). Numbers in parenthesis refer to line numbers of the original text on the tablet.

(1) The beginning of instructions being made by the hereditary prince, local prince, god's father, god's beloved, ear of the six great mansions, the mouth *that* brings peace to the entire land, mayor[1], vizier, Ptah-hetep, the noble.

He said before the Majesty of the King of Upper and Lower Egypt, Isesi[2], living forever, "When you grow old *you* become
(2) infirm. The flesh fails through weakness. What is old is new. Strength comes to grief because the heart beats slowly. The mouth is silent and has no voice. The eyes are dim. The ears are deaf. The heart is inert, weary every day.
(3) The mind is neglectful and cannot remember yesterday. Bone suffers from old age. The nose is blocked and not breathing. It is painful to stand or to sit. Good things become bad things. All tastes perish. What
(4) old age does to men is bad in all things.

"May your humble servant be ordered to choose a successor[3]. Allow me to elevate my son in my place, teaching him about the words of those who listened to the counsels of the distinguished men of former times.
(5) Noble men work for the ancestors. Therefore they will act for you as well. Distress will be eliminated from *your* subjects and Egypt[4] will work for you."

His Majesty said, "Teach him about the words from the past before you retire[5]. Then he will acquire the
(6) character of the children of the great ones. He who heeds (these words) will gain access to all righteousness and what he says will not produce satiety."

Translation

The beginning of the precepts[6] written by the hereditary prince, local prince, god's father, god's

(7) beloved, *ear of the six great mansions,* mouth that brings peace to the entire land, mayor, vizier, Ptah-hetep, the noble, to instruct the ignorant about knowledge and the rectitude of good words as beneficial for him who heeds, but as

(8) *detrimental for him who* disobeys them.

Notes:

1. literally "overseer of the town."
2. Djedkare Isesi was the 8th king of the 5th Dynasty, ruling from about 2365 BC to2322 BC.
3. literally "make a staff of old age."
4. literally "the two banks (of the Nile)."
5. literally "before you sit."
6. literally "maxims of good words."

Chapter 5

Translation Details

Front Side

The first line is the actual inscription taken from the photographs displayed previously, but enlarged for clarity. The image has been reversed left-to-right to make translating easier. Some of the images have been photoshopped for clarity.

The second line is the transcription based on Alan Gardiner with a few exceptions.

1) Because the tablet is based on the stela, if there is a significant conflict between the tablet and the stela fragments, the stela fragments are used as the source and the affected signs are underlined.

2) Signs missing from the tablet but included in the stela fragments are included and underlined.

3) If a missing, or lost, sign can be reasonably deduced from the context it is included and overlined.

The third line is the transliteration, using the transcription in line two as the source. Words, or parts of words, missing in the transcription are written in light italics.

The remaining lines are a direct translation of the text, along with footnotes offering further explanation or clarification.

1) Words missing from the original text are in italics.

2) In the translation, words are listed in the same order as shown in the transcription with sentences normally being written Verb-subject-adjectives-object-adjectives.

3) Words added for clarity in English are in parentheses. Forms of the verb "to be," not normally included in Egyptian, are included in their English language position in the translation.

Line 1

ḥ3t-sp 3	*ḥrw*	*ḫʿ*	*ḥr*	*nst.f*	*nbty*	*wḥm*	*mnw*	*ḥr-n-nbw*	*shri*	*t3wy*

Regnal year 3,[1]

Horus, appearing

upon throne his;

Two Ladies, repeating monuments; Golden Horus, brings peace

(to the) two lands;

1. Alan Gardiner opined that the  should properly be written as  and further that "it is quite unusual to find the date thus immediately preceding the full titulary." An examination of the stela fragment appears to show that the stela originally began with the kings titulary, starting with the common expression . Apparently the decision was made at a later time to add the date to the monument, so the *ʿnḫ* was erased and replaced with the *ḥ3t-sp 3*, which had to be shortened to fit the space.

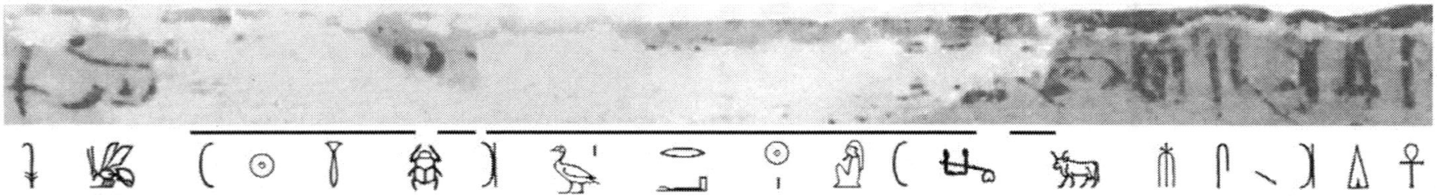

nsw-bity *w3ḏ-ḫpr-rꜥ* *s3* *rꜥ* *k3-ms* *di ꜥnḫ*

King of Upper and Lower Egypt,
Wadj-kheper-*Re*; *Son* *(of)* *Re*, Kamose, given life,

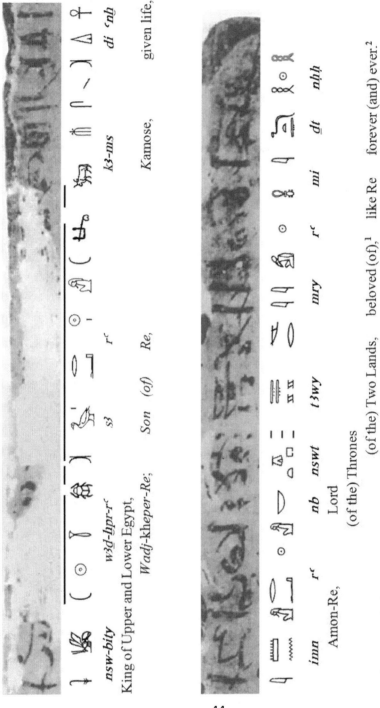

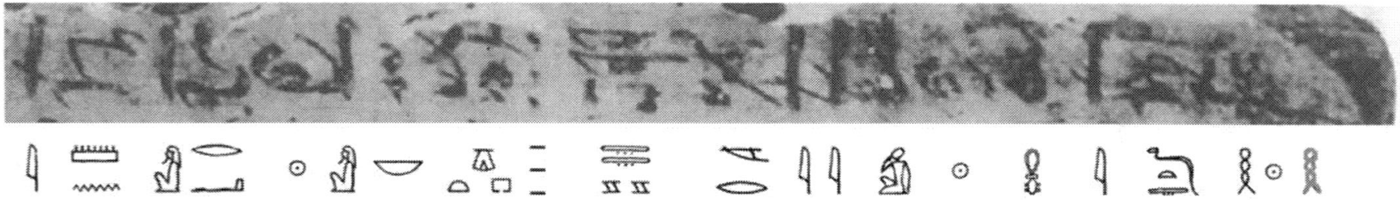

imn *rꜥ* *nb* *nswt* *t3wy* *mry* *rꜥ* *mi* *ḏt* *nḥḥ*

Amon-Re, Lord
(of the) Thrones
(of the) Two Lands, beloved (of),[1] like Re forever (and) ever.[2]

1. "beloved of" refers to Amon-Re.
2. "like Re forever and ever" refers back to "given life."

Line 2

nsw ***nḫt*** ***m-ẖnw*** ***wst*** ***k3-ms*** ***di ꜥnḫ ḏt***

King victorious inside (of) Thebes, Kamose, given
life forever,

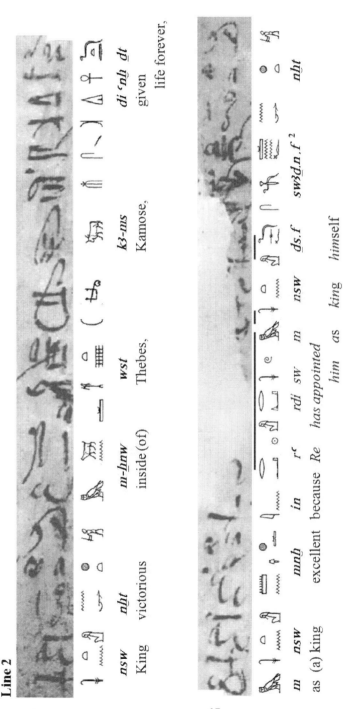

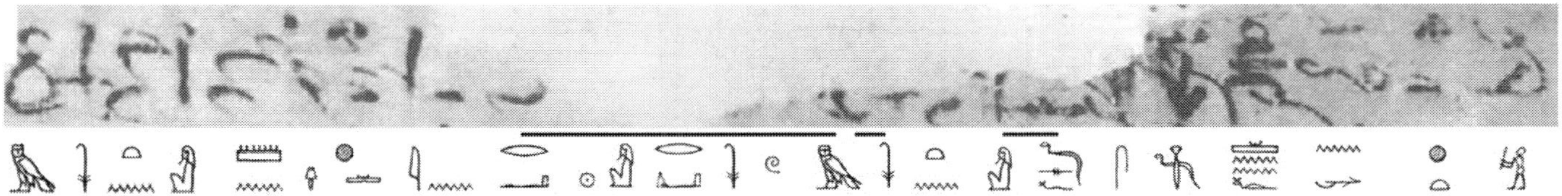

m ***nsw*** ***mnḫ*** ***in*** ***rꜥ*** ***rdi sw*** ***m*** ***nsw*** ***ḏs.f*** ***sw3ḏ.n.f*** [2] ***nḫt***

as (a) king excellent because *Re* *has appointed*
him *as* *king* *him*self
(and) has bequeathed
to him strength

1. Gardiner states that the second ***n*** is superfluous.

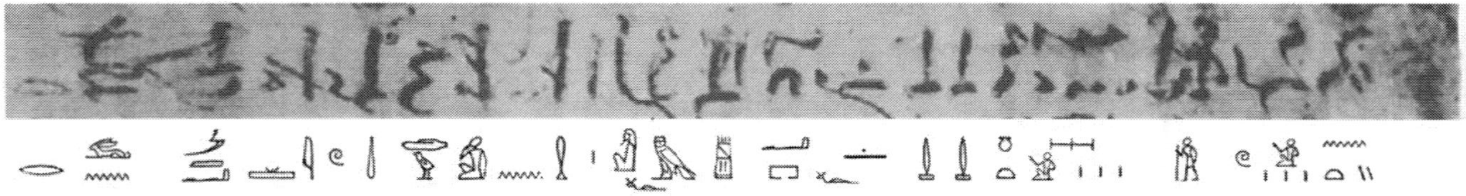

r wn m3ˁ iw[2] *mdw . n ḥm . f m ˁḥ . f n ḏ3ḏ3t srw nty*

as being true.[1] Spoken by majesty

his in palace

his to (the) counsel (of) noblemen who

1. "as being true" > "indisputable" or "veritable"
2. ***iw*** is an emphatic and not generally translated (see a grammar for its use).

Line 3

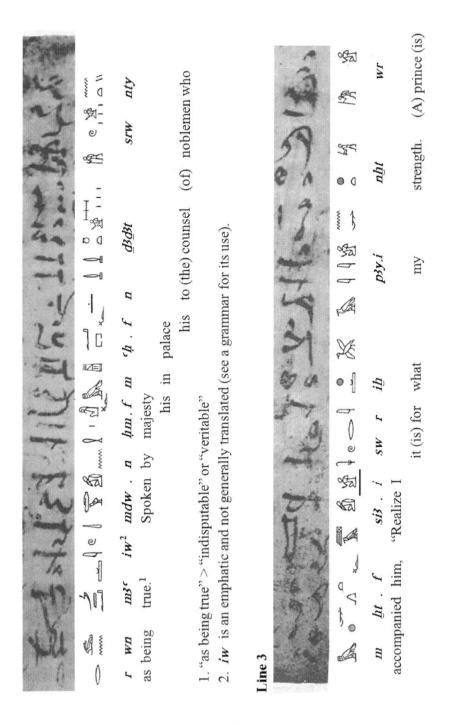

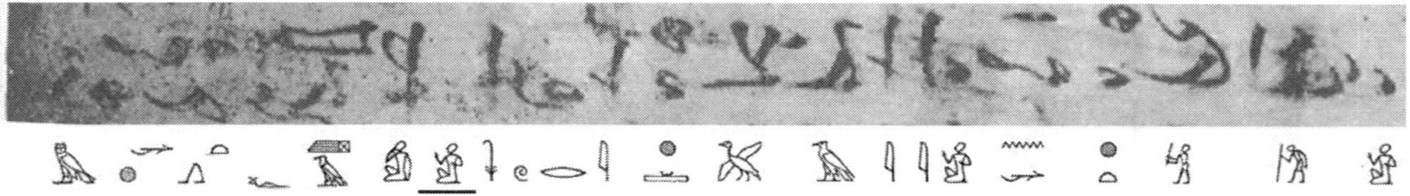

m ḫt . f si3 . i sw r iḫ p3y.i nḫt wr

accompanied him, "Realize I

it (is) for what my strength. (A) prince (is)

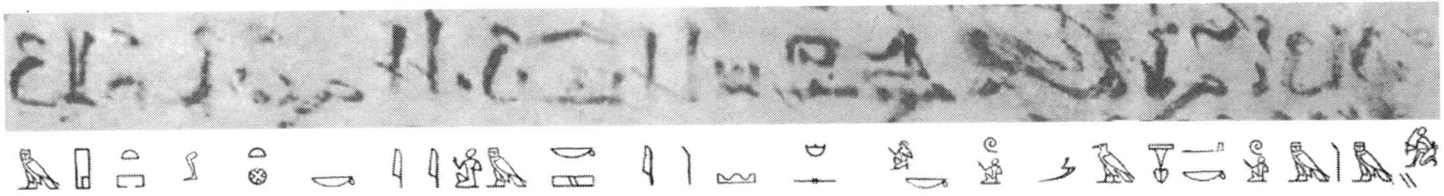

m *ḥwy-wꜥrt* *ky* *m* *kši* *ḥms* *kwi* *smꜣ*[1] *kwi* *m* *ꜥꜣm*

in Avaris (and) another (is) in Kush, (and) am seated I. Am united I with (an) Asiatic

1. The initial *s* of *smꜣ* is missing from the text.

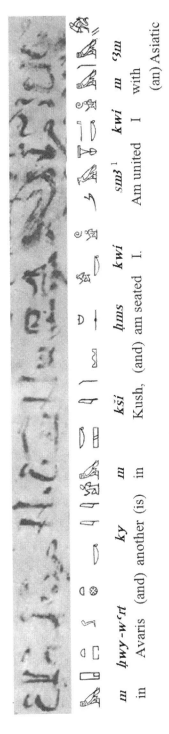

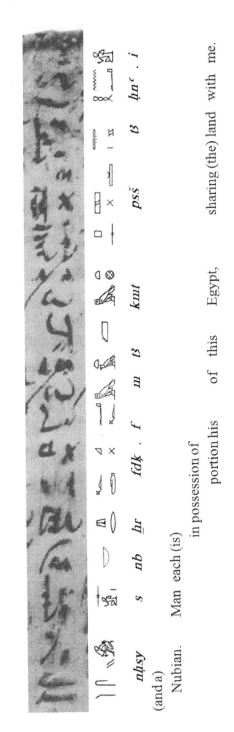

nḥsy *s* *nb* *ẖr* *fdḳ . f* *m* *tꜣ* *kmt* *psš* *tꜣ* *ḥnꜥ . i*

(and a) Nubian. Man each (is) in possession of portion his of this Egypt, sharing (the) land with me.

Line 4

nn *sni . i* *sw* *šꜣʿ* *r* *ḥwt-ptḥ* *mw*[1] *n* *kmt* *mʿk*

Cannot pass through

I it down to Memphis (on the)

water of Egypt. Behold,

1. Gardiner states that both the *mw* and *n* are doubtful.

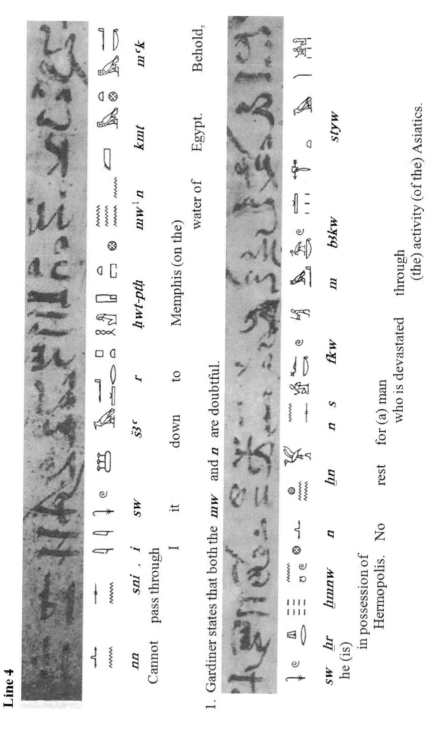

sw *ẖr* *ḫmnw* *n* *ẖn* *n* *s* *fkw* *m* *bꜣkw* *styw*

he (is)

in possession of

Hermopolis. No rest for (a) man

who is devastated through

(the) activity (of the) Asiatics.

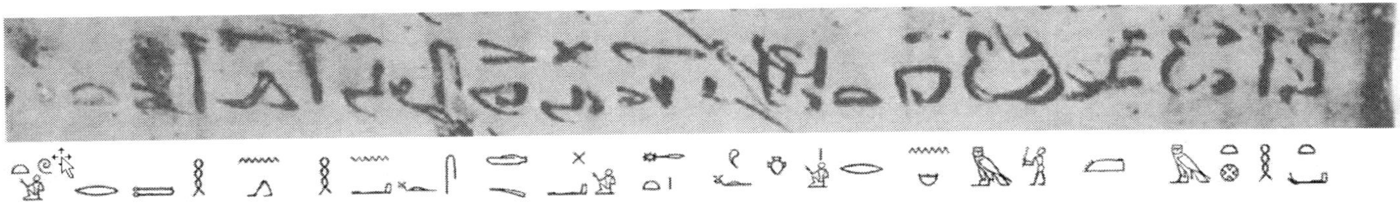

tw.i r *ṯḥn* *ḥnʿ . f* *sḏ . i* *ẖt . f ib.i r* *nḥm* *ḫmt* *ḥt*

I (am) to engage with him. Will slit open[1] I belly his. Desire my (is) to deliver Egypt (and) smite[2]

1. literally "break open"
2. *ḥwi* is "smite" but it seems to be the most reasonable option.

Line 5

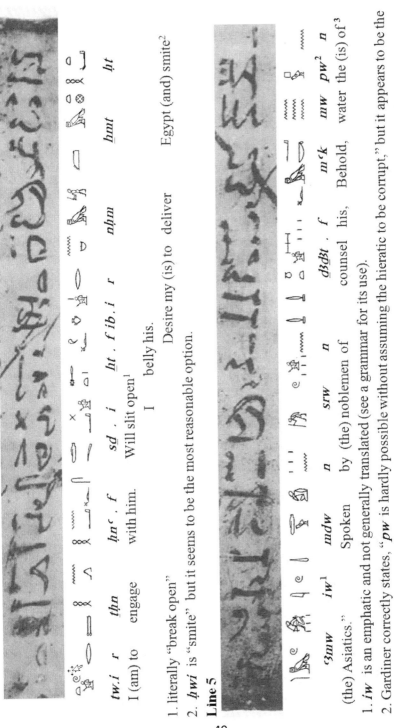

ʿ3mw *iw*[1] *mdw* *n* *srw* *n* *ḏ3ḏ3t . f* *mʿk* *mw* *pw*[2] *n*

(the) Asiatics." Spoken by (the) noblemen of counsel his, Behold, water the (is) of[3]

1. *iw* is an emphatic and not generally translated (see a grammar for its use).
2. Gardiner correctly states, "*pw* is hardly possible without assuming the hieratic to be corrupt," but it appears to be the only reasonable option.
3. "the water is of" > "the water belongs to"

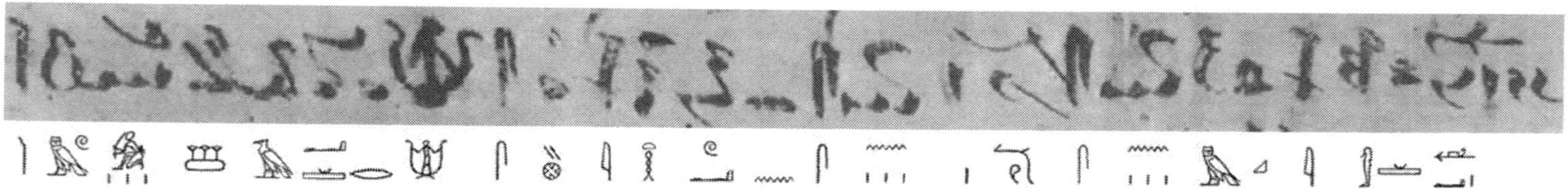

ʿ3mw *š3ʿ* *r* *ḳis* *itḥw . n . sn* *ns . sn* *m* *ḳi* *wʿ*

(the) Asiatics beginning at Cusae." Drew out by them tongues their all together[1],

1. "They drew out their tongues all together" > "They spoke with one voice"

Line 6

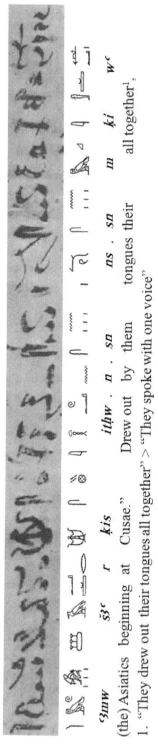

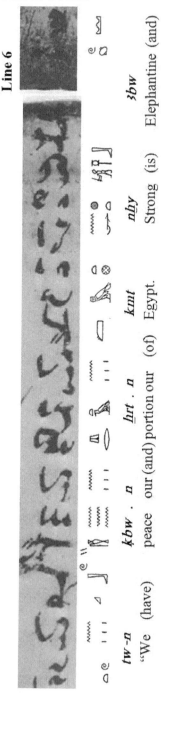

tw -n *ḳbw . n* *ẖrt . n* *kmt* *nẖy* *3bw*

"We (have) peace our (and) portion our (of) Egypt. Strong (is) Elephantine (and)

ḥry-ib *ḥnᶜ* *n* *šᶾᶜ* *r* *ḳis* *skᶾ* *tw* *n.n*

(the) middle

(is) together with us as far as Cusae. Plows one [2] for us

1. The first *n* appears to be superfluous.
2. When the subject of a sentence is "one" it is usually best translated as a passive sentence.

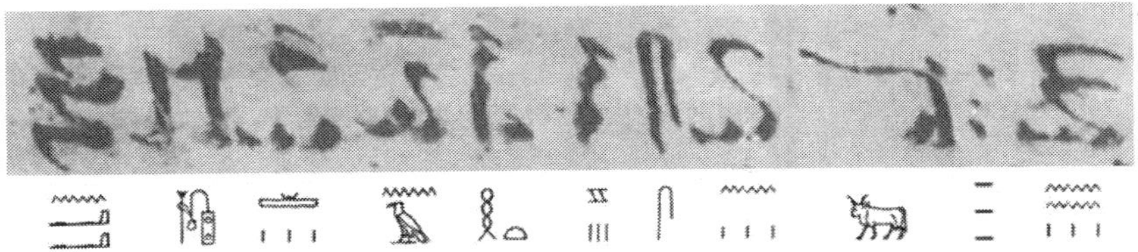

This text was inserted below line 6.

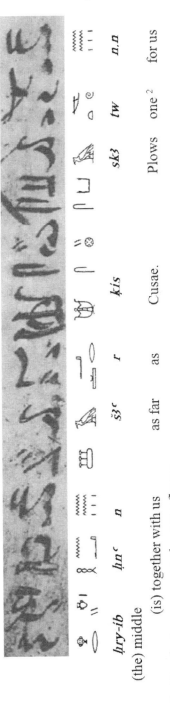

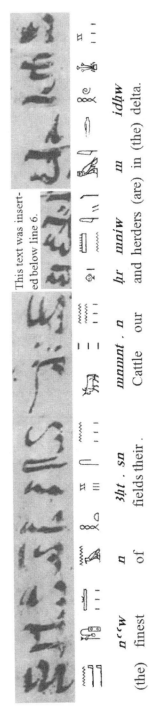

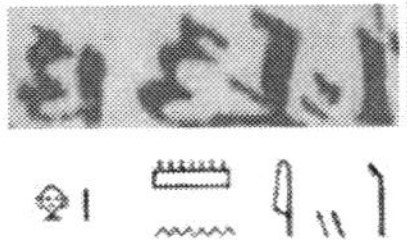

nᶜᶜw *n* *ᶾḥt . sn* *mnmnt . n* *ḥr* *mniw* *m* *idḥw*

(the) finest of fields their . Cattle our and herders (are) in (the) delta.

bdt *h3b* *r* *rrtw* *n* *n* *ṯt* *nmnmt* . *n* *n* *dp*

Emmer (is) sent to swine our . Not taken (are) cattle our by (the) crocodile.

Line 7

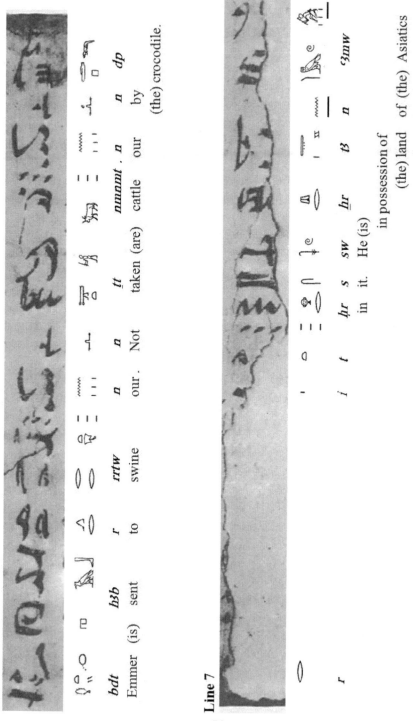

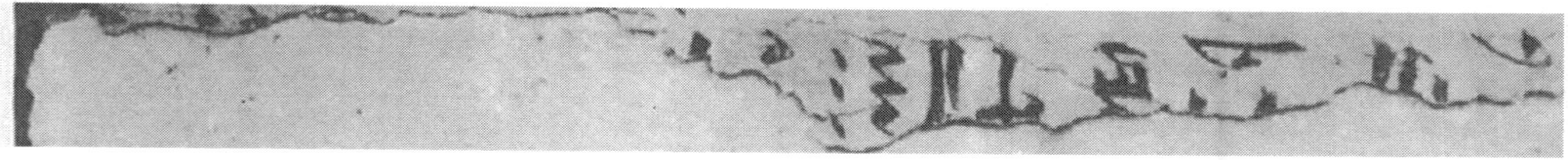

r *i* *t* *ḥr* *s* *sw* *ẖr* *t3* *n* *ˁ3mw*

in it. He (is) in possession of (the) land of (the) Asiatics

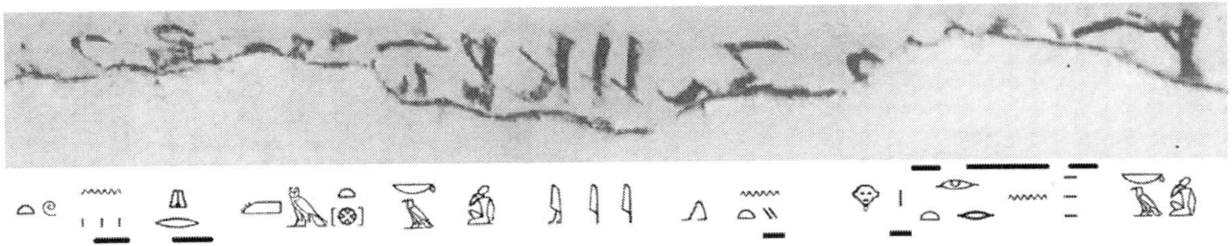

tw-n ẖr kmt k3 ii nty ḥr irt r . n k3

(and) we (are) in possession of Egypt. Then comes someone on act*ing* *against* us, then

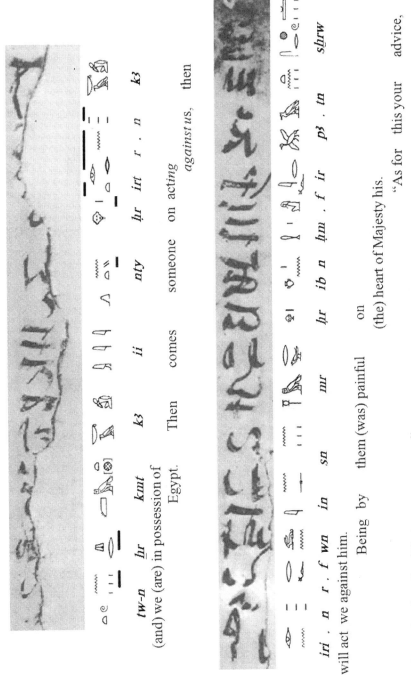

iri . n r . f wn in sn mr ḥr ib n ḥm . f ir p3 . tn sẖrw

will act we against him. Being by them (was) painful on (the) heart of Majesty his. "As for this your advice,

1. "being by them" > "their very presence"

Line 8

(This part of the story is missing from both the tablet and the stela fragments.)

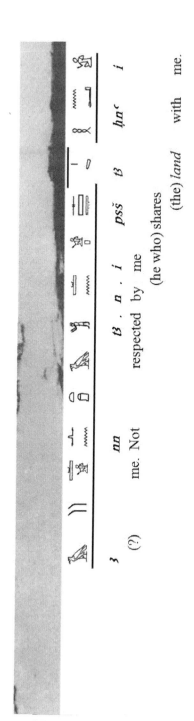

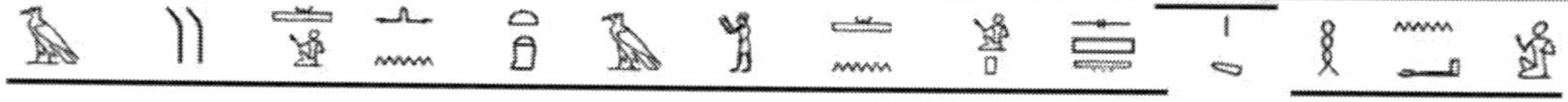

ꜣ *nn* *tꜣ . n . i* *psš* *tꜣ* *ḥnꜥ* *i*

(?) me. Not respected by me

(he who) shares

(the) *land* with me.

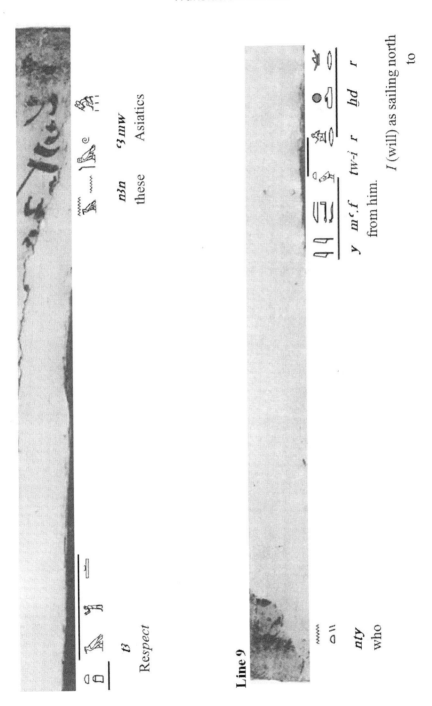

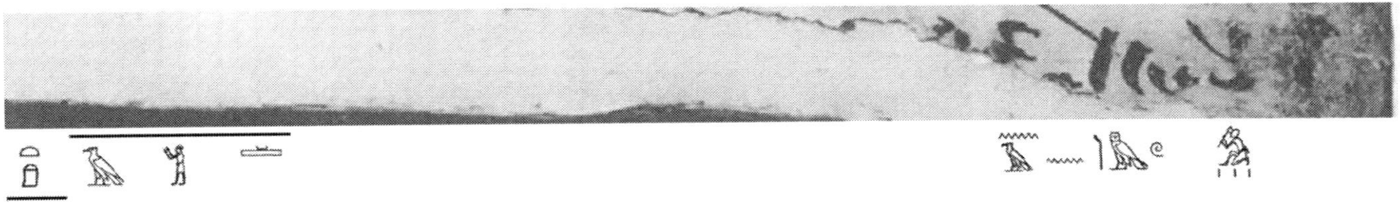

t3 Re*spect*

n3n these

ꜥ3mw Asiatics

Line 9

nty who

*y m*ꜥ*.f* from him.

tw-ỉ r *I* (will) as

ḫd sailing north

r to

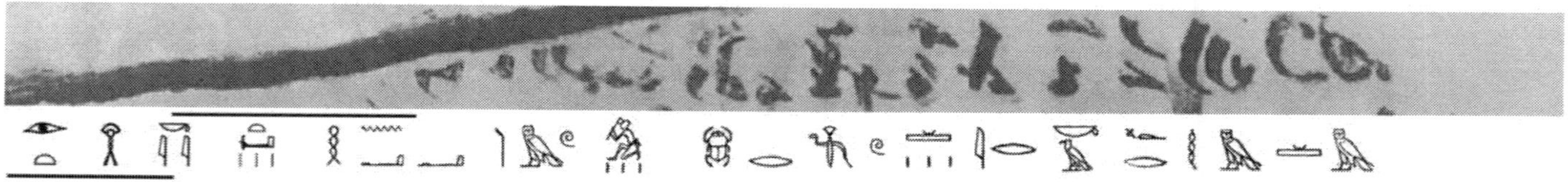

irt *skywt* *ḥnꜥ* *ꜥ3mw* *ḫpr* *w3ḏw* *ir* *k3.f* *r* *nḏm* *m*

do batt*le* *with* (the) Asiatics. Will occur good fortune.

If

thinks he

about relief from

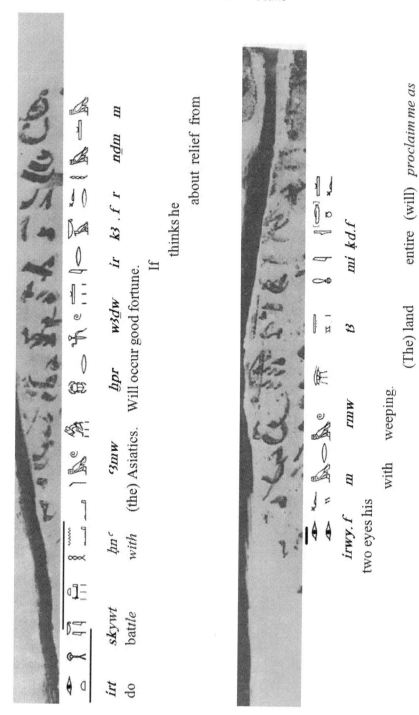

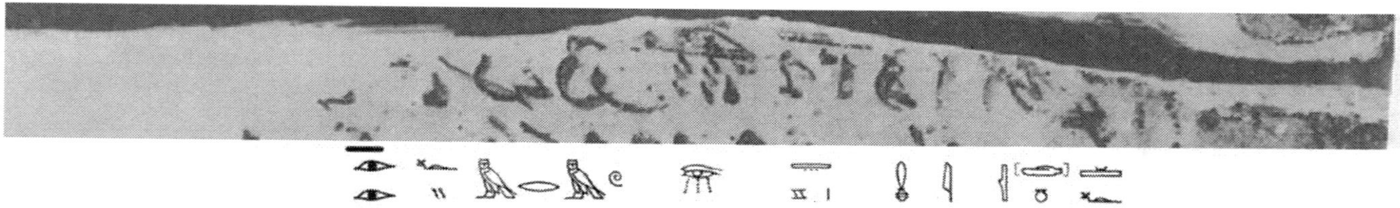

irwy.f *m* *rmw* *t3* *mi* *ḳd.f*

two eyes his

with weeping.

(The) land entire (will) *proclaim me as*

Line 10

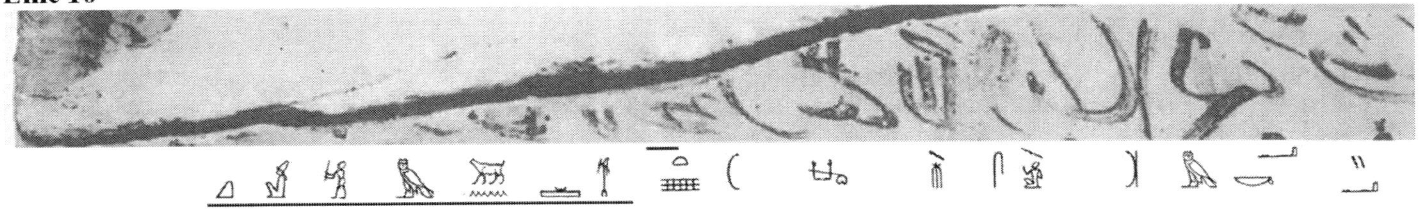

ḥḳ3	*m*	*nw*	*wst*	*k3-ms*	*mꜥkty*
*rul*er	in				
	(the) inside (of)		Thebes	Kamose,	protector

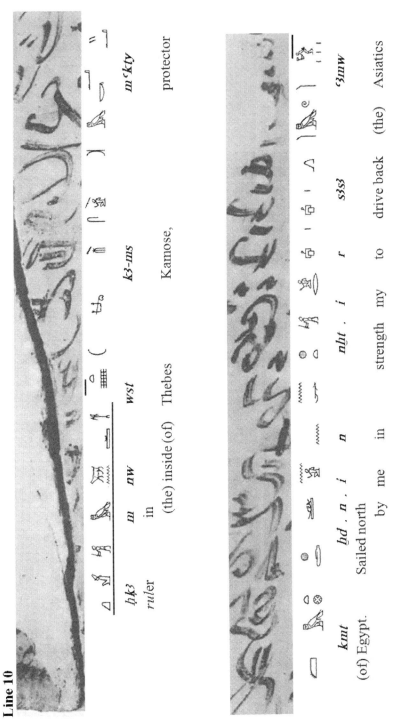

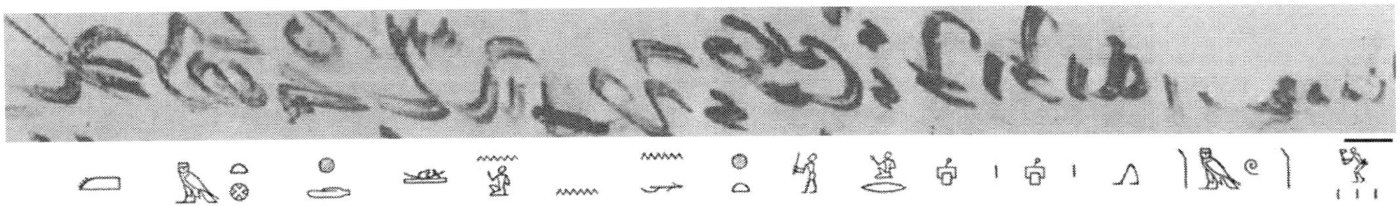

kmt	*ḫd . n . i*			*n*	*nḫt . i*		*r*	*s3s3*		*ꜥ3mw*
(of) Egypt.	Sailed north									
	by	me		in	strength	my	to	drive back	(the)	Asiatics

m *wḏ* *imn* *mtr* *sḫrw* *mšʿ . i* *ḳn*

as
commanded
Amun, eminent (of) counsels. Army my valiant (was)

Line 11

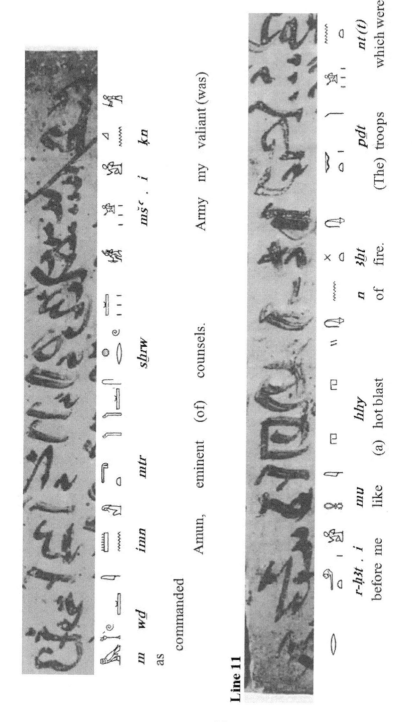

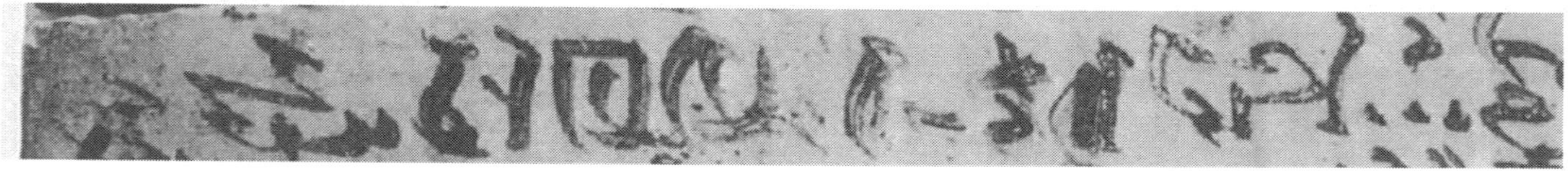

r-ḥ3t . i *mu* *hhy* *n* *3ḫt* *pḏt* *nt (t)*

before me like (a) hot blast of fire. (The) troops which were

md̠3yw *m* *ḥrt* *ṯ3r . n* *r* *hhy* *styw*

(the) Medjay (were) those on top (of) (the) cabin[1] our to search for (the) Asiatics (and)

1. "the cabin" is the cabin of the boat.

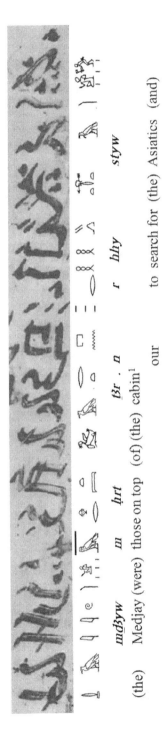

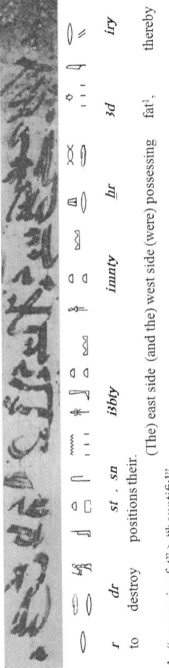

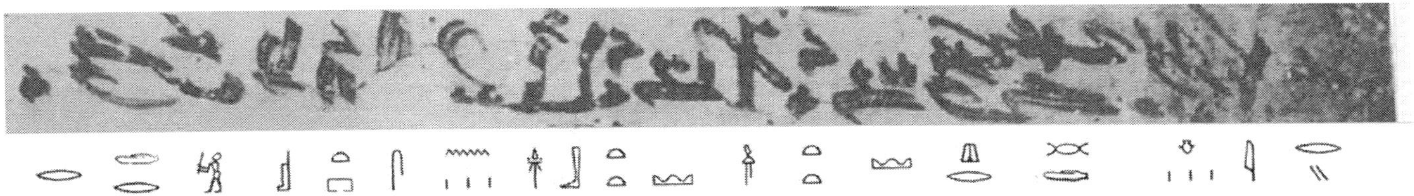

r *dr* *st . sn* *i3bty* *imnty* *ẖr* *3d* *iry*

to destroy positions their. (The) east side (and the) west side (were) possessing fat[1], thereby

1. "possessing fat" > "bountiful"

Line 12

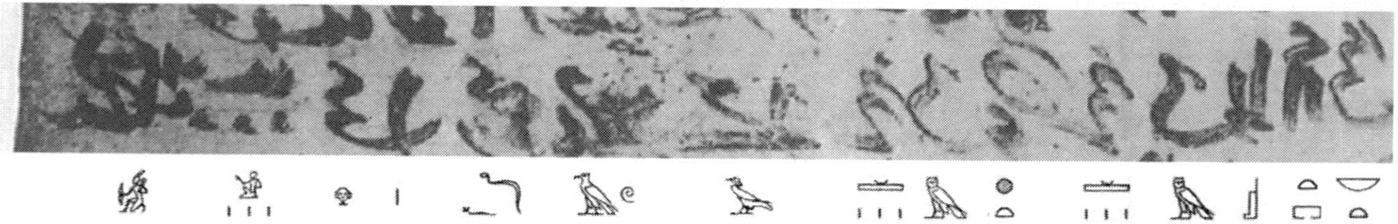

*mš*ʿ *ḥr* *d̠ßw* ʿ*ḳw* *m* *ḫ̱t* *m* *st* *nbt*

(the) army (was kept) in provisions (of) food with things from everywhere.

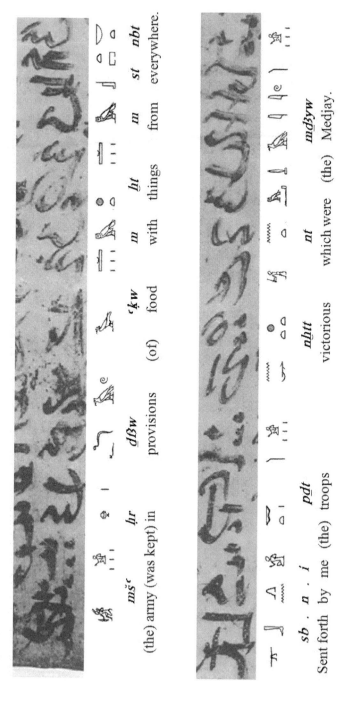

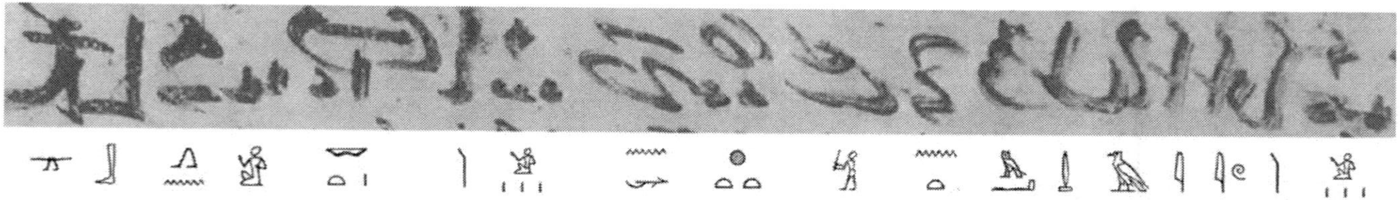

sb . *n* . *i* *pd̠t* *nḫ̱tt* *nt* *md̠ȝyw*

Sent forth by me (the) troops victorious which were (the) Medjay.

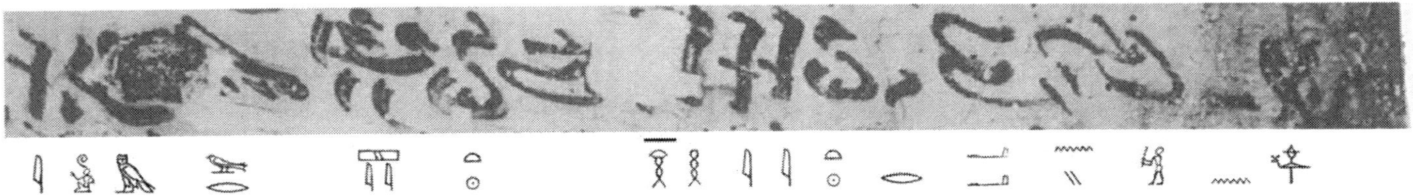

iw.i	*m*	*wršyt*	*ḫr*	*wḏyt*	*r*	*ʿʿny*		*n*	*ḫsf*
I (was)	as	one spending the day	(on an)	expedition	to	entrap	(and)	to	punish

Line 13

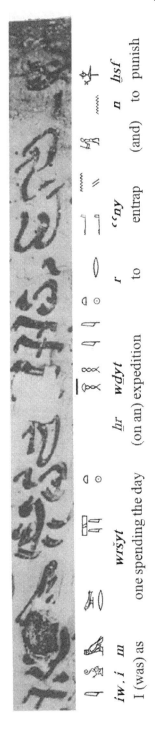

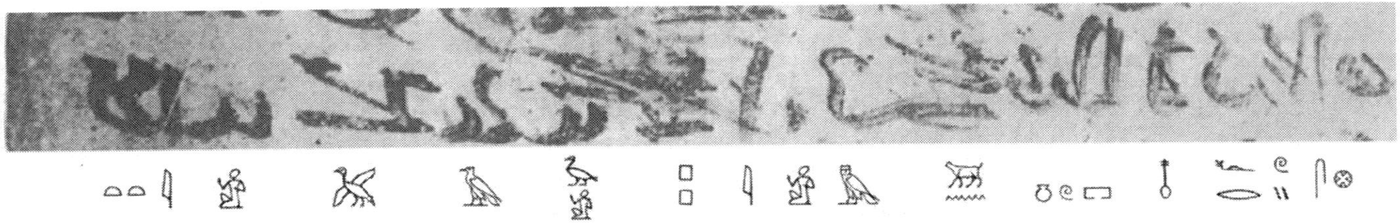

tti	*p3*	*s3*	*ppi*	*m-ḫnw*		*nfrwys*
Teti	the	son (of)	Apepi	in (the) inside	(of)	Nefrusi

nn rdi.i whi . f šnʿy . n . i ʿ3mw btn n kmt

(did) not permit

I to escape him, being restrained

by me. (The) Asiatic disrespector of Egypt,

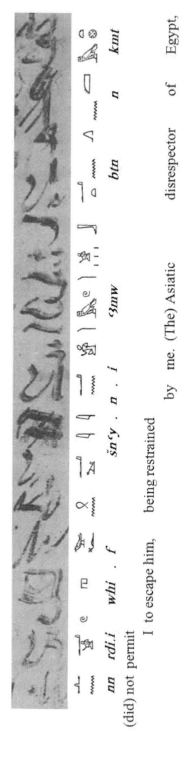

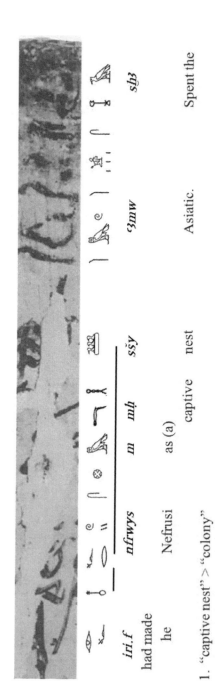

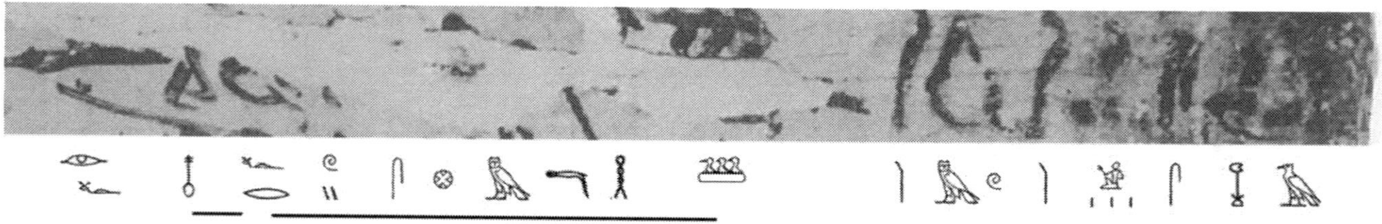

iri.f nfrwys m mḥ sšy ʿ3mw sẖ3

had made

he Nefrusi as (a)

captive nest Asiatic. Spent the

1. "captive nest" > "colony"

Line 14

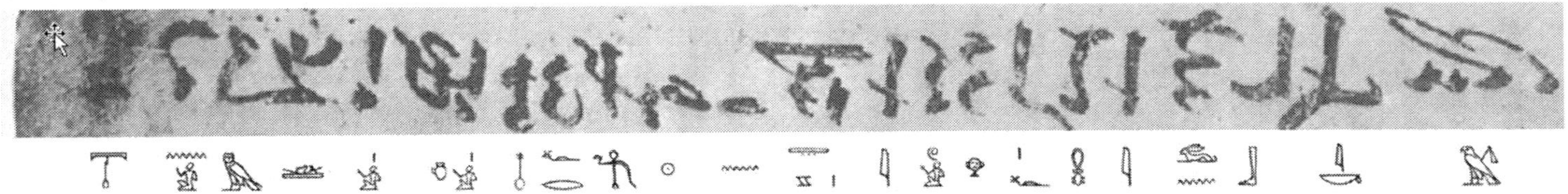

sḫꜣ . n . i m dpt . i ib . i nfr ḥḏ n tꜣ iw . i ḥr . f mi wn bik

night by me in ship my.
Heart my (was) happy.
(When) brightness (was) in
(the) land [1], I (was) on him like being (a) falcon.

1. “brightness was in the land” > “daylight arrived”

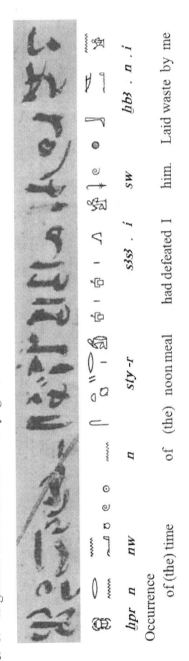

ḫpr n nw n sty -r sꜣsꜣ . i sw ḫbꜣ . n . i

Occurrence
of (the) time of (the) noon meal had defeated I him. Laid waste by me

sbty . f — walls his.

smꜣ . i — Killed I

rmṯ . f — people his.

rdi.i hꜣ ḥmt . f — Caused I to come down wife his

Line 15

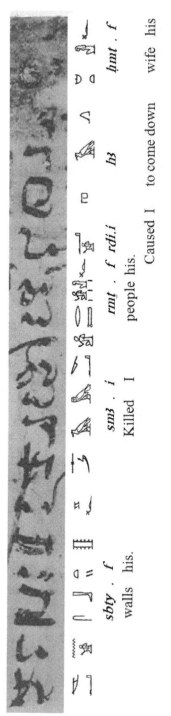

r mryt — to (the) river bank.[1]

mšʿ . i mi wn mꜣiw ḫr ḥꜣḳt — Soldiers my (were) like being lions with prey

1. "come down to the river bank" > "surrender"

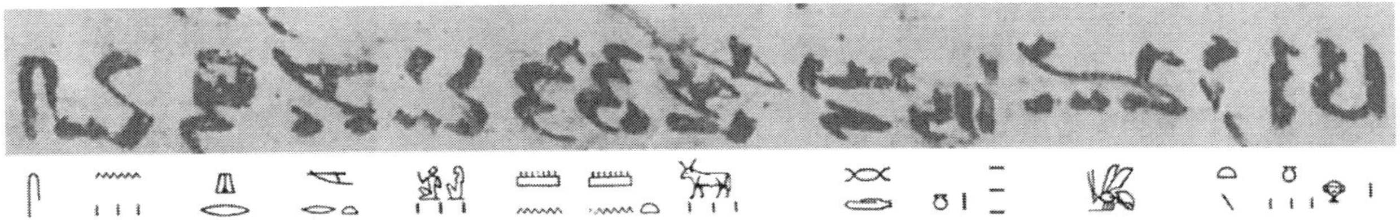

sn *ḫr* *mrt* *mnmnt* *ꜣd* *bit* *ḥr*

their , carrying off servants, cattle, fat (and) honey.

Through

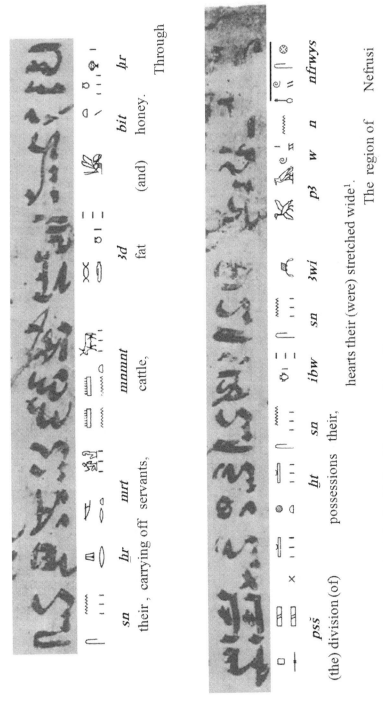

psš *ḫt* *sn* *ibw* *sn* *ꜣwi* *pꜣ* *w* *n* *nfrwys*

(the) division (of) possessions their,

hearts their (were) stretched wide[1].

The region of Nefrusi

1. “their hearts were stretched wide” > “they were happy”

Line 16

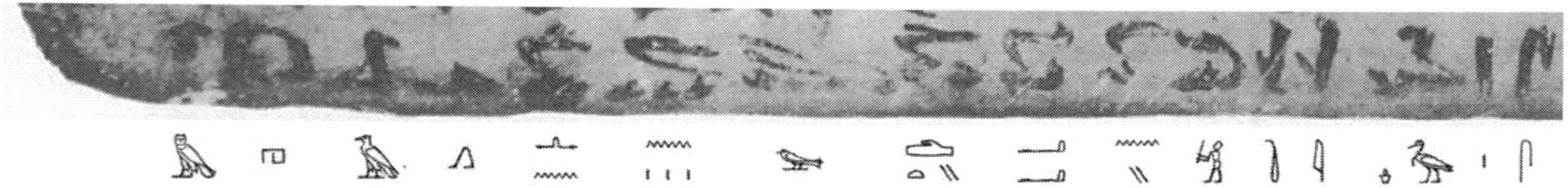

m *ḥ3* *nn* *n* *wr d*[1] *ˁˁny* *ti* *b3* *s*

(was) as fallen. (Were) not we weary (or) restrained. Lo spirits (were) caused

1. Instead of , Gardiner transcribed the hieratic as .

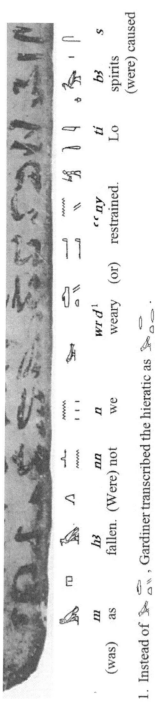

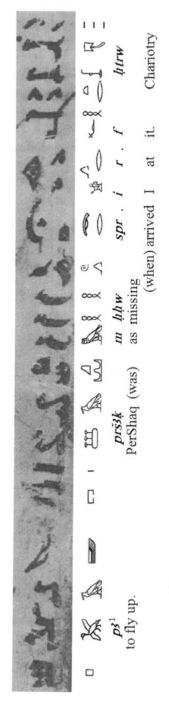

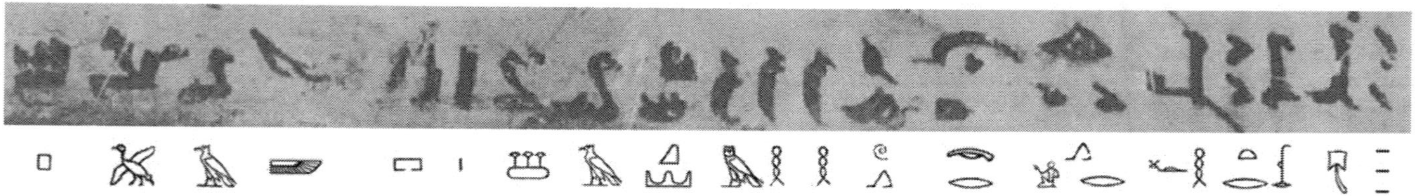

p3[1] *prš3ḳ* *m* *ḥḥw* *spr* . *i* *r* . *f* *ḥtrw*

to fly up. PerShaq (was) as missing (when) arrived I at it. Chariotry

1. Instead of , Gardiner transcribed the hieratic as .

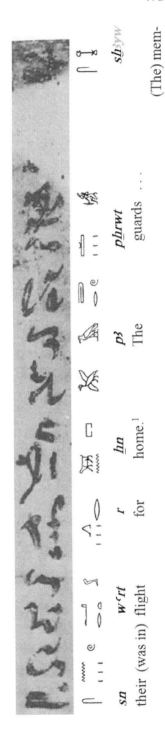

sn	*wʿrt*	*r*	*ḫn*	*pꜣ*	*pḫrwt*	*sḫꜣyw*
their (was in)	flight	for	home.[1]	The	guards . . .	(The) mem-

1. Could also mean “inside”

Line 17

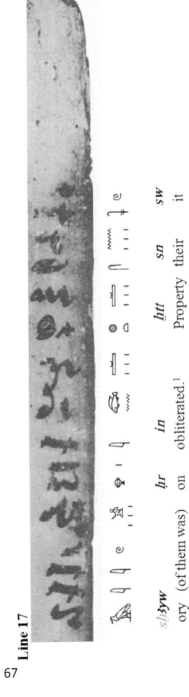

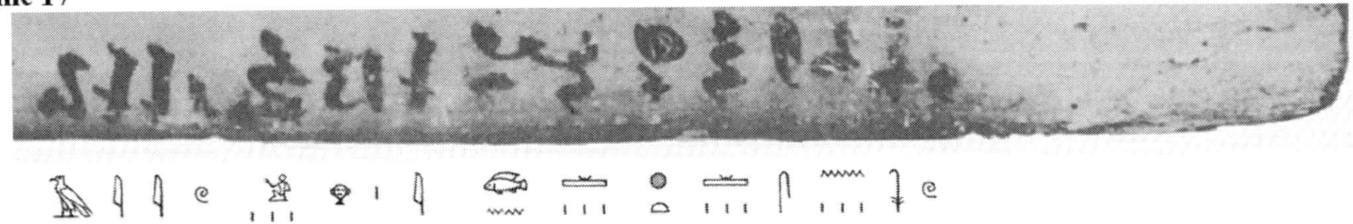

sḫꜣyw	*ḥr*	*in*	*ḫtt*	*sn*	*sw*
ory (of them was)	on	obliterated.[1]	Property	their	it

1. The translation of this sentence is very uncertain.

Back Side

The first line is the actual inscription taken from the photographs displayed previously, but enlarged for clarity. The image has been reversed left-to-right to make translating easier. Some of the images have been photoshopped for clarity.

The second line is the transcription based on Gaston Maspero with the exception that obvious errors have been corrected.

The third line is the transliteration, using the transcription in line two as the source.

The remaining lines are a direct translation of the text, along with footnotes offering further explanation or clarification.

1) Words missing from the original text, when they can be inferred, are in italics.

2) In the translation, words are listed in the same order as shown in the transcription with sentences normally being written Verb-subject-adjectives-object-adjectives

3) Words added for clarity in English are in parentheses. Forms of the verb "to be," not normally included in Egyptian, are included in their English language position in the translation.

Line 1

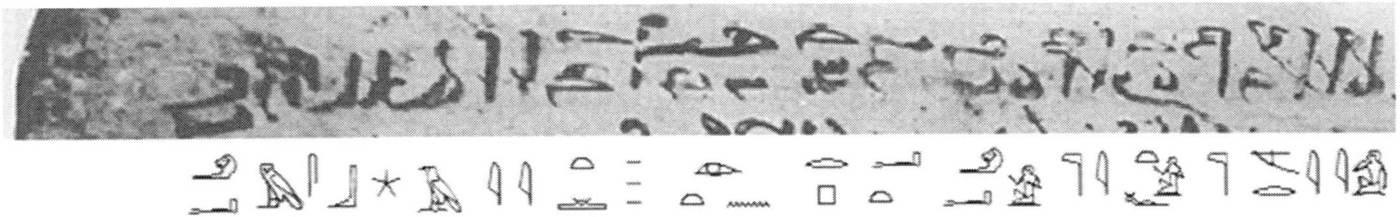

ḥ3t-ʿ m sb3yt irt . n rpʿt ḥ3ty-ʿ nṯr it nṯr mry

(The) beginning of instructions being made by
(the) hereditary prince,
local prince,
god's father, god's beloved,

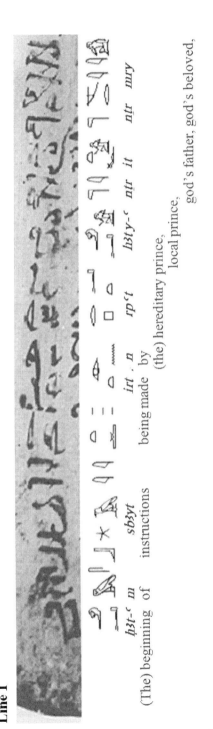

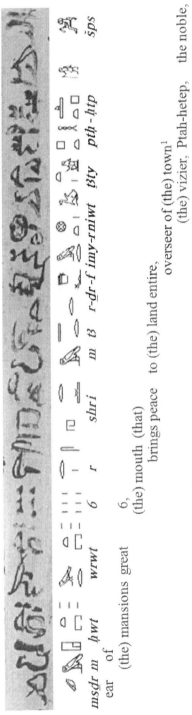

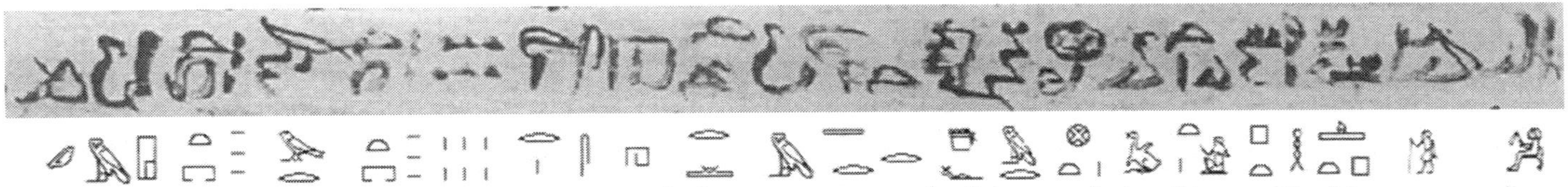

msḏr m ḥwt wrwt 6 r shri m t3 r-ḏr-f imy-r niwt ṯ3ty ptḥ-ḥtp šps

ear of
(the) mansions great 6,
(the) mouth (that)
brings peace to (the) land entire,
overseer of (the) town[1]
(the) vizier, Ptah-hetep, the noble,

1. "overseer of the town" > "mayor"

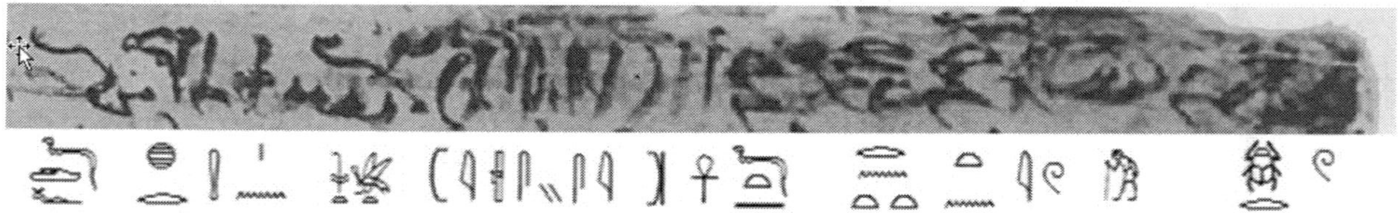

ḏd.f *ḥr* *ḥm.n* *nsw-bity* *issi*¹ *ʿnḫ* *ḏt* *rntt* *tn* *iwi* *ḫprw*

Says he, before (the) Majesty of (the) King of Upper and Lower Egypt, Isesi, living forever, "When you (are) growing old (you) become

1. Djedkare Isesi was the 8th king of the 5th Dynasty, ruling from about 2365 BC to 2322 BC.

Line 2

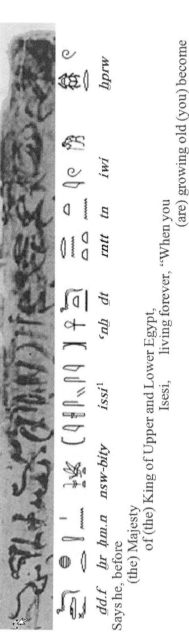

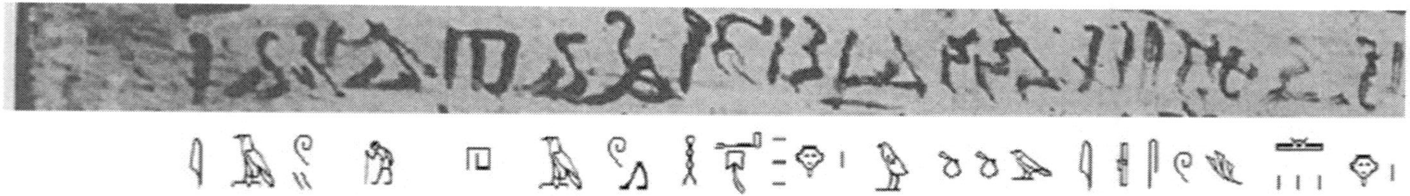

ȝwi *hȝwi* *ḥ ʿ* *ḥr* *wgg* *isw* *ḥr*

infirm.¹ Fails flesh through weakness. What is old (is) as

1. *ȝwi* is literally "old aged"

m3wy *pḥty* *3ḳ* *n* *wrd* *ib* *r* *gr* *n* *ḫrw* *f*

new. Strength (has) come to grief
because is weary (the) heart. [1]
(The) mouth (is) silent
(and has) not voice its.

1. “the heat is weary” > “the heart beats slowly”

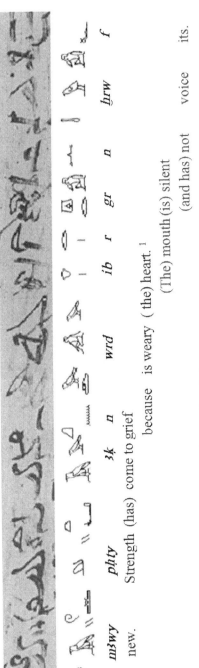

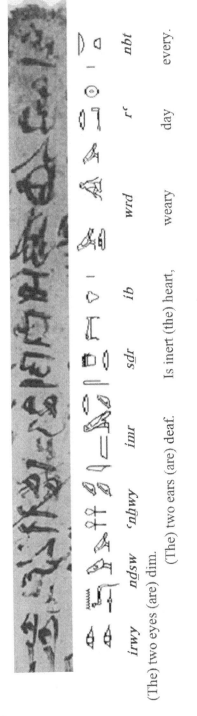

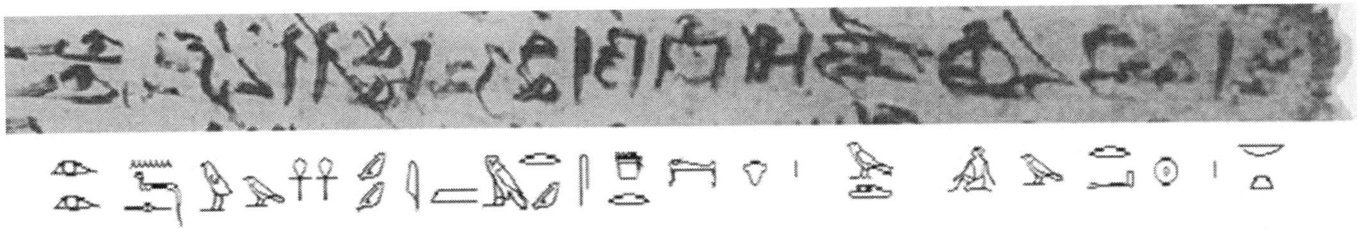

irwy *nḏsw* *ʿnḫwy* *imr* *sḏr* *ib* *wrd* *rʿ* *nbt*

(The) two eyes (are) dim.
(The) two ears (are) deaf. Is inert (the) heart, weary day every.

Line 3

ib *mhw* *n* *sh3* *n f* *sf* *ks* *mn* *nf* *i3w*

(The) mind (is) neglectful (and) not remember this yesterday.

(The) bone (is) suffering from this old age.

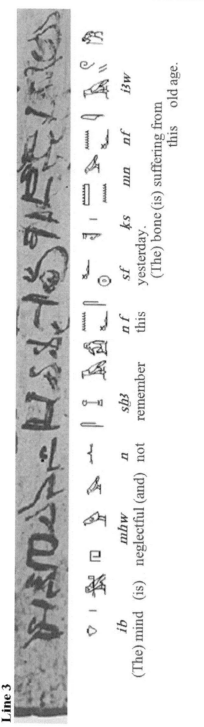

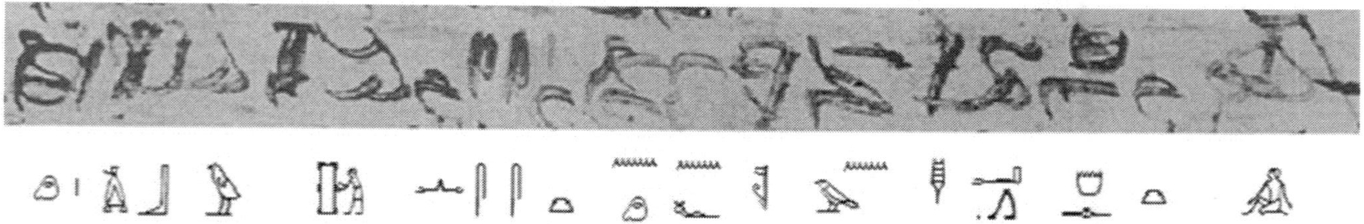

fnd *db3w* *n* *sstn* *nf* *ksn* *ʿḥʿ* *ḥmst*

(The) nose (is) blocked (and) not breathing. This (is) painful to stand (or) to sit.

bw - nfr *ḫpr* *m* *bw - bin* *dpwt* *nbt* *ȝk* *st* *irt*

Good things become as bad things. Tastes all perish they. What does

Line 4

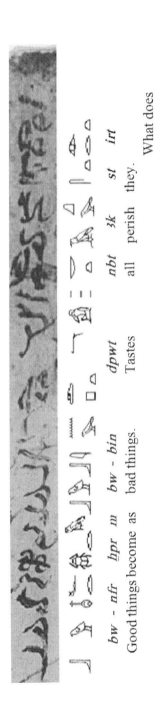

iȝw . n *rmṯ* *bin* *m* *ḫt* *nbt* *m-m* *wḏ* *tw n*

old age to men (is) bad in things all. Wherewith (will) order one[1] of

1. When the subject of a sentence is "one" it is usually best translated as a passive sentence.

b3k-im *irt* *md* *i3w* *rdi tu* *ʿḥʿ* *s3.i* *m* *st.i* *sb3*

your humble servant

to make (a) staff of old age?[1] (Will) allow one[2] (me)

to elevate son my in place my, teaching

1. “make a staff of old age” is an idiom for “choose a successor.”
2. When the subject of a sentence is “one” it is usually best translated as a passive sentence.

Line 5

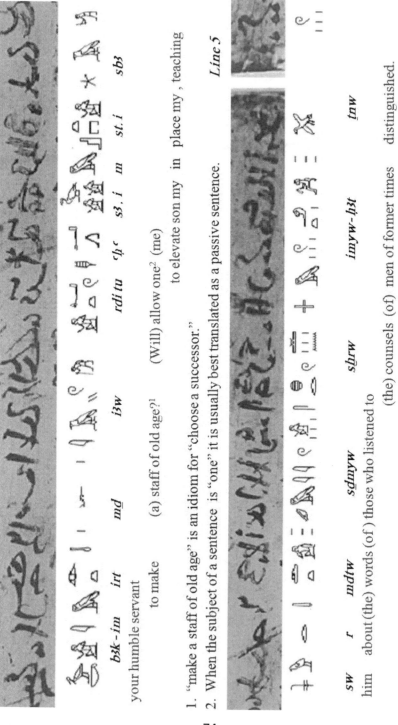

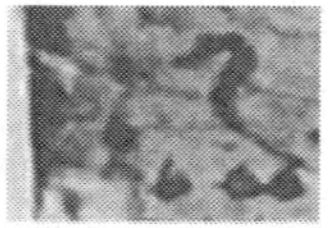

sw *r* *mdtw* *sḏmyw* *sḫrw* *imyw-ḥ3t* *ṯnw*

him about (the) words (of) those who listened to

(the) counsels (of) men of former times distinguished.

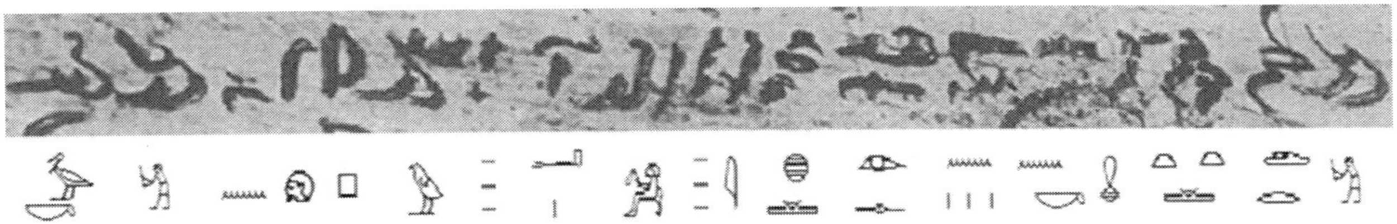

b3k . n tpw - ͑ špsw iḫ iri . sn n . k mitt dr

Work for (the) ancestors noble men.

Therefore will act they for you as well. Will eliminate

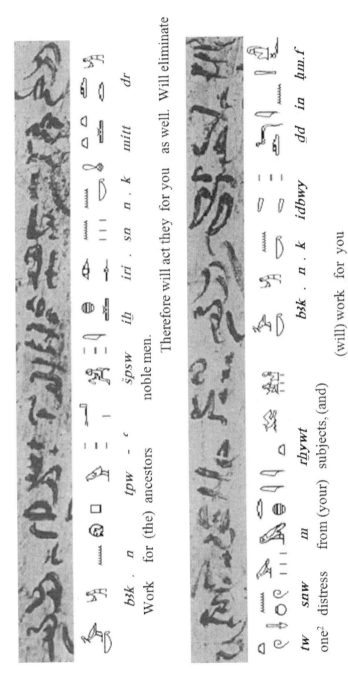

tw snw m rḫywt b3k . n . k idbwy ḏd in ḥm.f

one[2] distress from (your) subjects, (and)

(will) work for you

(the) two banks.[1]" Words spoken

by Majesty his

1. "the two banks" > "Egypt"
2. When the subject of a sentence is "one" it is usually best translated as a passive sentence.

sb3 *ir . k* *sw* *r* *mdt* *ẖr* *ḥ3tt* *ḏr* *ḥmst . k* *iḫ* *iri.f*

"Teach you him about (the) words from (the) past before sit you.[1] Then will acquire he

1. "before you sit" > "before you retire"

Line 6

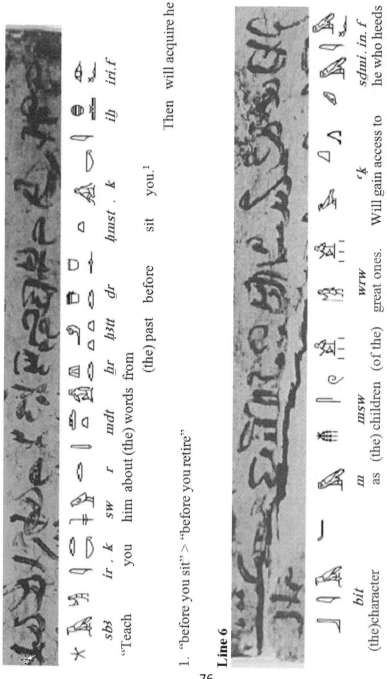

bit *m* *msw* *wrw* *ʿḳ* *sḏmi . in. f*

(the)character as (the) children (of the) great ones. Will gain access to he who heeds

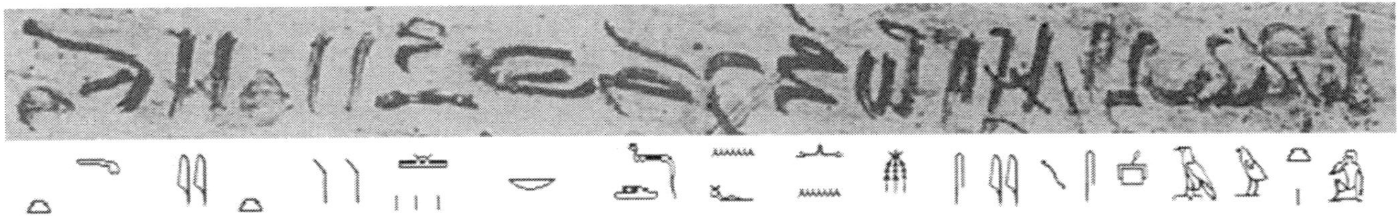

mtyt *nb* *ḏd .n .f* *nn* *msy* *s3wt*

righteousness all

(and) said by him[1]

(will) not produce satiety."

1. "said by him" > "what he says"

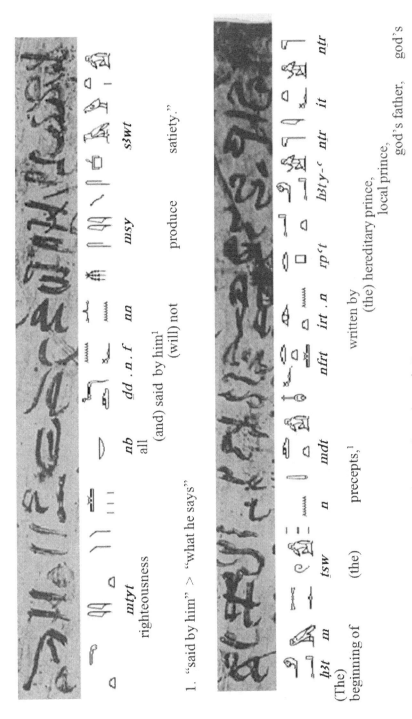

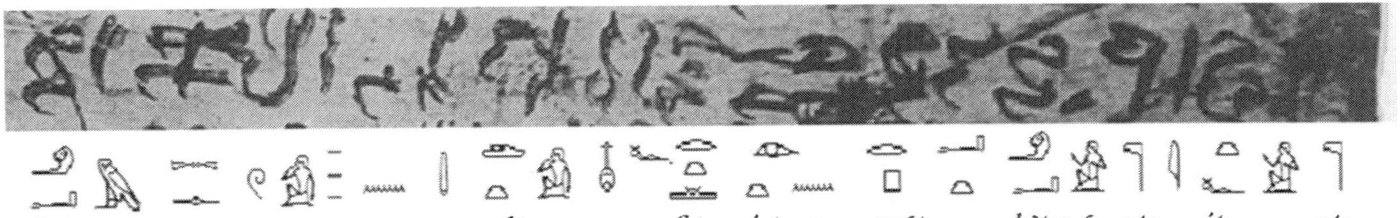

ḥ3t *m* *ṯsw* *n* *mdt* *nfrt* *irt .n* *rpʿt* *ḥ3ty-ʿ* *nṯr* *it* *nṯr*

(The)
beginning of (the) precepts,[1] written by

(the) hereditary prince,

local prince,

god's father, god's

1. ***ṯsw n mdt nfrt*** is literally "maxims of good words."

Line 7

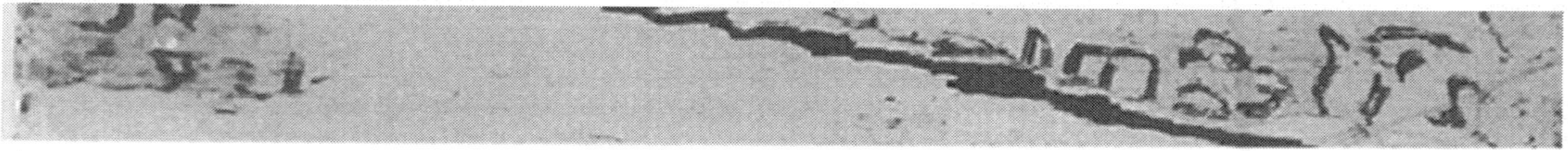

mry beloved, *ear of the 6 great mansions,*

r shr m t3 r-dr-f mouth (that) brings peace to (the) land entire,

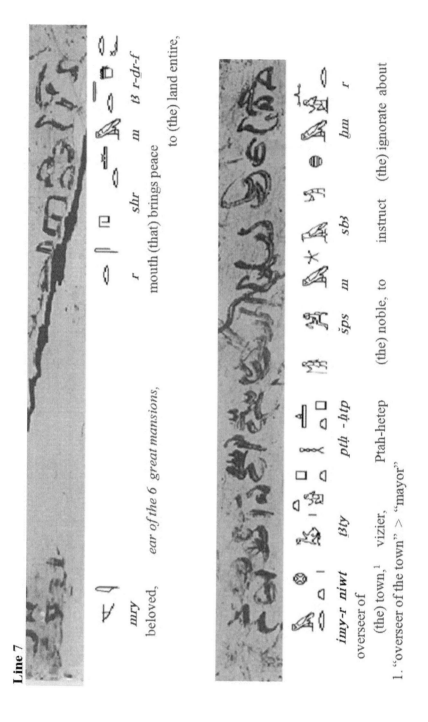

imy-r niwt overseer of (the) town,[1] *t3ty* vizier, *ptḥ-ḥtp* Ptah-hetep *šps* (the) noble, *m* to *sb3* instruct *ḫm* (the) ignorate *r* about

1. "overseer of the town" > "mayor"

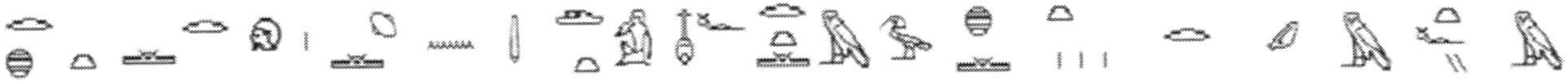

rḫt *r* *tp-ḥsb* *n* *mdwt* *nfrt* *m* *3ḫt* *r* *sḏmt.f* *m*

knowledge (and) about the rectitude of words good as beneficial for him who heeds (but) as

Line 8

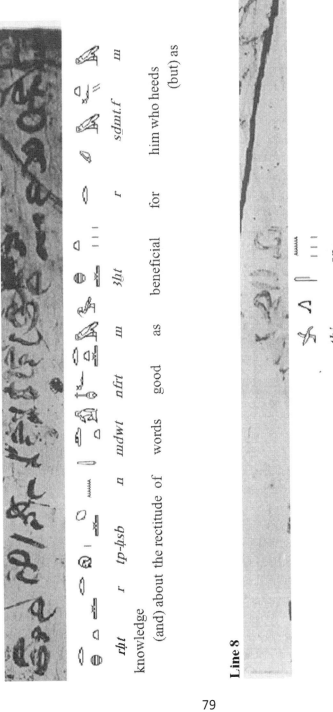

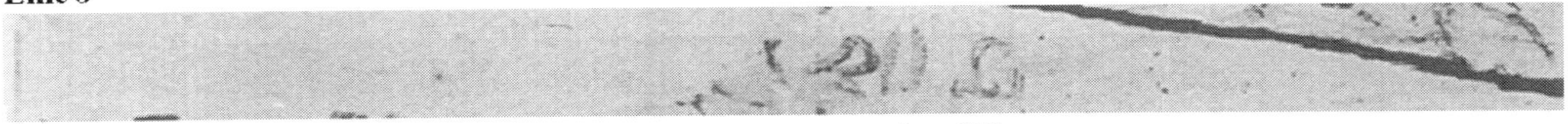

thi *sn*

detrimental for him who disobeys them.

Chapter 6

Kamose Stela 1

In 1932 and 1935 two fragments were found in the third pylon of Karnak temple during conservation work carried out by H. Cherrier which were found to be from a stela of King Kamose commemorating his victories over the Hyksos. These stela fragments fit together and mirrored much of the text on the Carnarvon Tablet. The combined size of the two fragments is 22 inches (56 cm) wide and 41 inches (104 cm) high. Based on comparisons with the text on the tablet it has been estimated that the original stela was about 80 inches (203 cm) wide. The height can only be guessed at. However the second Kamose stela (discovered in 1954) is 49 inches (125 cm) wide and 91 inches (231 cm) high. If used for camparison, a height for the first stela of between 91 inches (231 cm) and 160 inches (406 cm) would not be surprising. The fragments are currently in the Egyptian Museum in Cairo with the inventory number 11.1.35.1.

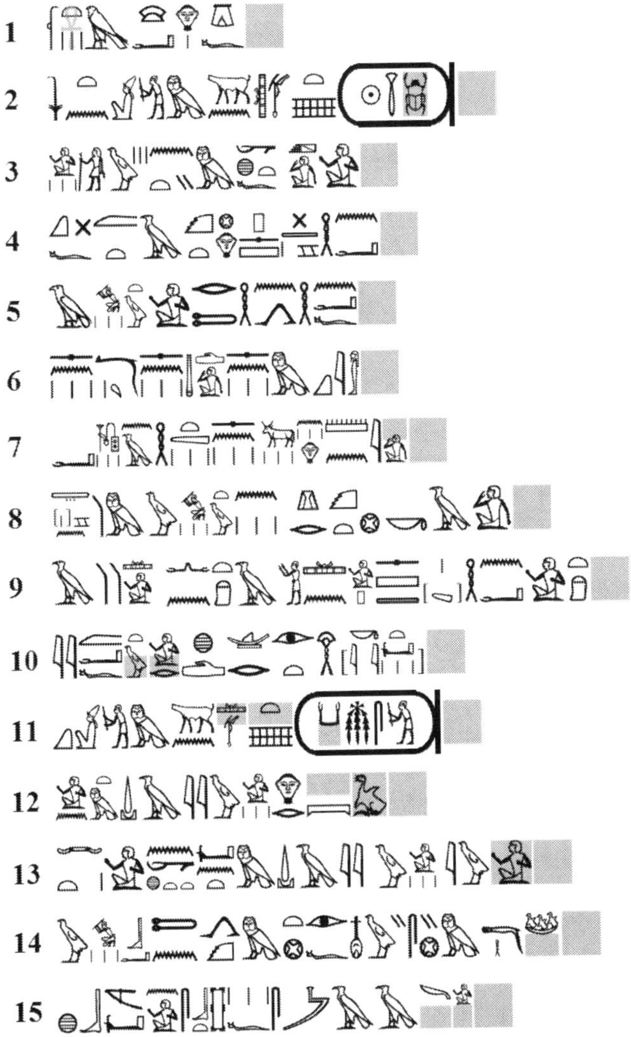

Bibliography

Breasted, James H. *Ancient Records of Egypt*, Chicago, University of Chicago Press, 1906.

Budge, E. A. W. *Facsimiles of Egyptian Hieratic Papyri in the British Museum*, London, 1910

Carnarvon, The Earl of and Howard Carter *Five Years' Explorations at Thebes.* London: Oxford University Press, 1912.

Engberg, Robert M. "The Hyksos Reconsidered." *Studies in Ancient Oriental Civilization No. 18.* Chicago: University of Chicago Press, 1939.

Gardiner, Alan H. "The Defeat of the Hyksos by Kamose: The Carnarvon Tablet, No.I." *JEA, Vol 3*, EES, 1916.

Gotsova, Velichka. "Political and Economic Relations Between Egypt and Hyksos at the End of the 17th Dynasty." *JES III*, 2010

Habachi, L. *The Second Stela of Kamose and his Struggle against the Hyksos Ruler and his Capital.* Bluckstadt: J.J. Augustin, 1972

Hankey, Julie. *A Passion for Egypt: Arthur Weigall, Tutankhamun and the 'Curse of the Pharaohs'.* London: Tauris Parke Paperbacks, 2007.

Helck, W. *Historisch-biographische Texte der 2. Zwischenzeit und neue Texte der 18. Dynastie.* Wiesbaden: 1975

Horne, Charles F. *The Sacred Books and Early Literature of the East.* New York: Parke, Austin, & Lipscomb, 1917.

James, T. G. H. *Howard Carter : The Path to Tutankhamun*. London: Tauris Parke Paperbacks, 2001.

Jequier, G. *Le Papyrus Prisse et ses variantes (Papyrus de la Bibliotheque Ntionale (No 183 a 194), Papyrus 10371 et 10435 du British Museum, Tablette Carnarvon au Musee du Caire).* Paris : 1911.

Bibliography

Maspero, Gaston. "L'Ostracon Carnarvon et le Papyrus Prisse." *Recueil de Travaux Relatifs à la Philologie et à l'Archéologie , Vol. XXXI.* 1909.

Moller, G., *Hieratische Palaographie: I, Alt- und Mittelhieratisch; II, Neuhieratisch.* Leipzig: 1909.

Newberry, Percy. E. "Notes on the Carnarvon Tablet No. I." *Proc. S.B.A., vol. 35.* 1913.

Posener, G., "Notes de transcription." *RdE 33*. 1981.

Weill, R. "Les Hyksos et la Restauration Nationale." Paris. 1911.

NOTES

NOTES

NOTES

NOTES

NOTES

Books by Bill Petty

Hieroglyphic Sign List: Based on the Work of Alan Gardiner

The Names of the Kings of Egypt: The Serekhs and Cartouches of Egypt's Pharaohs, along with Selected Queens (with Kevil L. Johnson)

Hieroglyphic Dictionary: A Middle Egyptian Vocabulary

Egyptian Glyphary: A Sign List Based Hieroglyphic Dictionary of Middle Egyptian

English to Middle Egyptian: A Reverse Hieroglyphic Dictionary

Understanding Hieroglyphic Inscriptions: An Introductory Course to the Ancient Egyptian Language

Ahmose: An Egyptian Soldier's Story

Luxor: Gods, Grit and Glory (editor and co-author)

Books from Museum Tours Press

“The Essentials”

These are five books that anyone with a serious interest in ancient Egypt will want to keep readily available.

Hieroglyphic Sign List: Based on the Work of Alan Gardiner by Bill Petty – 5½" by 8½", soft cover, 132 pages. This book contains the 800 Hieroglyphic signs that one is most likely to encounter. Each sign is shown along with its origin, transliteration, use and meaning. $14.95.

Hieroglyphic Dictionary: A Middle Egyptian Vocabulary by Bill Petty – 5½" by 8½", soft cover, 181 pages. Containing almost 5,000 unique entries, arranged alphabetically, this book emphasizes words found in historical inscriptions. Its unique organization, sorting words by their first two letters, make it exceptionally easy to use. $14.95.

The Names of the Kings of Egypt: The Serekhs and Cartouches of Egypt's Pharaohs, along with Selected Queens by Kevin Johnson & Bill Petty – 5½" by 8½", soft cover, 122 pages. This handy book contains the Horus names, Prenomens and Nomens for 300 Kings and 29 Queens of ancient Egypt. Its handy size and cost make it a must-have. $14.95.

Egyptian Glyphary: A Sign List Based Hieroglyphic Dictionary of Middle Egyptian by Bill Petty – 5½" by 8½", soft cover, 294 pages. A Glyphary™ is organized along the lines of a Hieroglyphic Sign List, but each sign is followed by a list of words, with definitions containing the selected sign. It has over 4,000 unique entries. $14.95.

English to Middle Egyptian Dictionary: A Reverse Hieroglyphic Vocabulary by Bill Petty – 5½" by 8½", soft cover, 296 pages. At last, here is a usable English to Egyptian dictionary. Containing about 8,000 entries, it has almost four times the number of words as Gardiner's vocabulary. $14.95.

More Books from Museum Tours Press

Urkunden Der 18. Dynastie by Kurt Sethe – 6" by 9", soft cover, 1,226 pages. Out of print for over 100 years, this is still one of the most highly referenced works in Egyptology. Available in four volumes with over 300 pages each, this facsimile edition contains the original German text and hand drawn hieroglyphs. $14.95 per volume.

"This set of 18th Dynasty Egyptian inscriptions is a classic which has been out of print for a number of years and even when found, fetches a hefty price. Now available in an affordable reprint, it can once again adorn the shelves of the interested layperson or scholar. Sethe's handwritten transcriptions of these historical texts add an extra layer of fullness to the study of this period." KJ 12/12

Understanding Hieroglyphic Inscriptions: An Introductory Course to the Ancient Egyptian Language by Bill Petty – 8" by 10", soft cover, 252 pages. This is a self-paced, introductory course to under-standing Egyptian hieroglyphs. With a minimum of grammar and a maximum of translation based on actual inscriptions, it is an excellent way to begin your quest to comprehend the ancient Egyptian language. $19.95.

"This book is perfect for anyone desiring an understandable tutorial. I took beginning hieroglyphs many years ago in Chicago. I wish this had been the textbook. Must have for any Egyptologist ... Amateur or pro." DB, 6/15

"Take advantage of Bill Petty's welcome addition to the excellent range of books already available for learning hieroglyphs." FB, 3/15

"The grammatical explanations are clear and concise. There are a lot of workbook-style exercises along the way." B, 7/14

"I enjoyed this course because I found the logical progression of concepts easy to follow. Each chapter builds on the previous one without stranding the reader. There are many exercises and the answers are included in an appendix for those of us who get stuck. ... (Egyptian is) a very complex language, with exceptions to the many rules. Bill Petty did a great job of describing the rules, when and how they are applied, and giving great examples. I highly recommend it." TH, 5/14

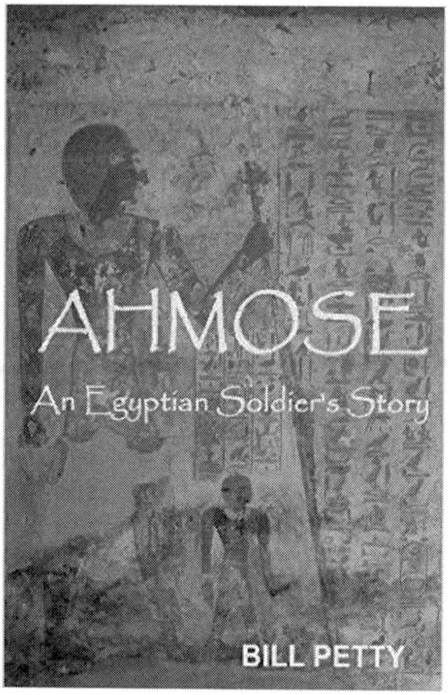

Ahmose: An Egyptian Soldier's Story by Bill Petty – 6" by 9", soft cover, 310 pages, over 100 illustrations, photographs and maps. An interpretive biography of the soldier, Ahmose, Son of Ibana. It includes a complete translation, with notes, of the autobiography that Ahmose, inscribed on the wall of his tomb in ElKab. $16.95.

"Ahmose, An Egyptian Soldier's Story should be must reading for everyone with an interest in the late-17th, early-18th dynasties." Kmt: A Modern Jounal of Ancient Egypt, Spring 2015

"Ahmose is a beautiful story – and thank you for writing it." AH, 4/15

"A fascinating glimpse into a life long ago. A must read for anyone who loves ancient Egypt." C, 3/15

"Here is a great opportunity to learn about the rise of the New Kingdom and the early pharaohs who were responsible for its success. Bill traces the life of a typical soldier and his family during this period. The maps are excellent and make the story so much easier to follow." FB, 3/15

"This book is a treasure-trove for the layman Egyptologist.

"Its first half is devoted to an historical reconstruction of the late 17th-early 18th Dynasties of Egyptian history ... . It is a tour-de-force exercise in multi-disciplinary historical writing.

"The book's second half contains: a free translation of the Ahmose inscription, a thorough-going translation and commentary, several ancillary historical sources critical to his discussion, a handy timeline, several family trees, an authoritative discussion of the Egyptian

military organization of the time, comments on the Egyptian calendar, a glossary of terms, bibliography, and index. In short, Petty has totally nailed it.

"Petty's military background comes on full-force in describing to us what an ancient Egyptian soldier's life truly was like". WC, 4/15

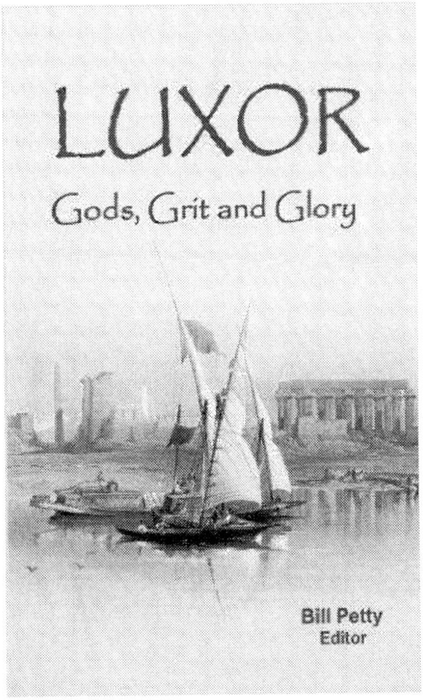

Luxor: Gods, Grit and Glory edited by Bill Petty – 5" by 8", soft cover, 450 pages. Consists of 25 short stories by 12 authors that trace the history of Luxor from prehistoric times to the present. Historical fiction at its best. $19.95.

"Wonderful read." TY, 11/15

"A very entertaining read." AC 9/15

"If you're a lover of ancient Egypt this book is a must read. It spans the history of the city of Luxor, Egypt with interesting and informative short stories that bring this fascinating town, its people and its history to life. The stories are of everyday people and not of the lofty biblical movie versions we're all so familiar with. I found the stories entertaining and completely absorbing." CG, 9/15

"A unique and engaging presentation of Egyptian history, told through the eyes of inhabitants of the times, through stories depicting actual events. For those of us not apt to pick up a thick book on Egyptology, yet are romanced by the times, "Luxor: Gods, Grit and Glory" provides rich and entertaining tales that weave the reader through this hypnotic era of history. A variety of authors contribute to the book, each with a voice that pulls the reader in, challenges one to turn the page." JB, 12/15

51293201R00058

Made in the USA
Lexington, KY
19 April 2016